VEGGIE
FAST
FOOD

VEGGIE
FAST
FOOD

GRUB STREET · LONDON

VEGGIE FAST FOOD
Page 6

Us, why and how? Answers to these and other questions, in addition to tips and tricks for fast and easy cooking.

SANDWICHES ETC.
Page 14

Here are all sorts of sandwiches to eat with your hands. Many also make an excellent snack to eat on the go.

CHIPS, FINGER FOOD ETC.
Page 54

If you're looking for an alternative to the traditional fast food side serving of chips, you'll find what you're after here. Not only will you see unusual creations such as feta cookies, but also revisited classics like sushi to tempt you.

BURGERS ETC.
Page 82

A fast food book won't work without burgers! So we give this much-loved and quintessential fast food a whole chapter filled with possibilities.

PIZZA ETC.
Page 108

Everybody loves pizza! Of course we do
too, and would like to show you a few
creative ways to make it. You will also
find meat-free recipes for tarte flambée
and lahmacun (Turkish pizza) here.

DIPS,
SAUCES ETC.
Page 128

Good fast food also needs matching
dips and sauces. Sometimes spicy,
sometimes fruity and sweet – there's
something to suit all tastes here.

BREAD ROLLS ETC.
Page 158

Everything needs to be fast and easy to
make. That's why our baked creations
spend most of their time in the oven,
and we make very few modifications to
the ingredients of our multi-purpose
dough.

DRINKS ETC.
Page 176

Because we don't want to leave you
thirsty with all these wonderful things,
we offer you recipes for the two classic
refreshments – cola and lemonade –
with a new look.

FOREWORD: US, WHY AND HOW?

What is the main reason for writing a cookbook? The answer is quite obvious: a love for cooking. What specifically led us to write a book on vegetarian and vegan fast food is the following story:

Clarissa had been following a meat-and fish-free diet for a long time, but she was accepting enough to fall in love with Florian. For him at the time, anything without meat was only a side dish, and fast food was a part of his daily life. However, Florian developed a great passion for cooking, and as he was naturally considerate of his new love, he acquired an insight into vegetarian cuisine and learnt to appreciate and enjoy it. Since their work often meant they could spend little time with each other, and as they didn't want to give up their evenings of cooking together and preparing homemade treats, they developed an inclination for fast food. In order to find more inspiration, Florian wanted to find a cookbook devoted to vegetarian fast food, but he was unsuccessful. So one thing led to another, and the result was this cookbook. In it both have immortalised their favourite recipes and dishes.

TOFU-FREE VEGETARIAN

When die-hard omnivores hear the word 'vegetarian', they immediately tend to think of tofu. And why would you blame them? It is quite usual for many recent converts to a vegetarian diet to replace sausages, meat and fish with tofu and other similar substitute products. As a result, fish fingers become tofu fingers, and spaghetti Bolognese is made with finely minced tofu. Why is this? With the huge number of vegetables and pulses, fruit and cheeses that are available to choose from, people should be able to cook wholesome and delicious food without having to use tofu or seitan.

That's why we dispense with them in our cookbook and show that variety is still possible. Fancy a sandwich? Try the version using crumbed oyster mushrooms (see recipe on page 49). Or simply replace the frank-furter in a hot dog with a carrot (see recipe on page 94). We hope you have fun trying. Bon appétit.

THE DEFINITION OF FAST FOOD

What is fast food? Put simply, it's food that's quick to prepare and easy to eat. The idea behind fast food is to simplify the intake of nourishment to suit our fast-moving times. A short lunch break can be more effective when holding a sandwich in your hand while you enjoy a stroll.

You can decide between a kebab, burger or curry on a whim, without having to put up with restaurant bookings, slow service or long waits. Whether you eat your food on the spot, while you walk, on a park bench, or take it home is up to you.

FAST FOOD AND VEGETARIANS

Fast food is becoming more popular every day, but changes are taking place. For decades, fast food chains monopolised the market, leaving us very little choice and very few alternatives. Over time, vegetarianism has become an increasingly popular lifestyle choice, while the desire for a healthy lifestyle has become stronger and, together with the trend for veganism, is now becoming firmly entrenched in society. So it is now inevitable that not only the big chains should offer vegetarian and vegan alternatives on their menus. More and more small and independent fast food establishments are offering meat-free and animal-product-free treats alongside their standard fare. Not only has this increased the variety now available, but also the demand for vegetarian and vegan fast food. The unhealthy image of fast food is slowly crumbling, and a craving for fast food need no longer come with a guilty conscience.

THE HISTORY OF FAST FOOD CULTURE

Excavations show that fast food restaurants existed as far back as thousands of years ago in ancient Pompeii. So-called *thermopolia* had clay pots set into recesses in a stone counter to keep ready-made meals of lentils, beans and peas warm for hungry customers. In other countries, such as China, hawkers were already selling the equivalent of today's takeaway meals.

Fast food underwent an upheaval during the Industrial Revolution, not only because there was less free time, but also because more women joined the workforce. Because there was often little time to prepare food at home, people would pick up quick, ready-made meals to take home with them. Given the increasing demand, a corresponding supply developed. An example of this is the horse-drawn lunch wagons that roamed around American industrial areas selling fast food.

VEGANISING

Even for vegetarians, cooking vegan meals can often be time-consuming, laborious and, consequently, off-putting. But often only minor changes are needed to make a dish that is one hundred per cent free of any animal products. To simplify this process, we offer the following tips and show you how to apply them to the recipes.

THE BASICS OF VEGANISING

Butter: A high-quality vegetable margarine makes a good substitute.

Milk and cream: There are now a large number of alternatives available on the market. The most common are milks and creams made from soya, oats and rice. As the typical soya milk products are somewhat bland, we recommend oat-based products.

Yoghurt: There isn't much choice here. Non-dairy alternatives made from soya can be found in most supermarkets. However, it should be noted that some types have a particularly sweet flavour and may not be suitable for savoury dips.

Mayonnaise: Egg-free mayonnaise is available from some supermarkets, well-stocked organic food and health food shops, and from mail-order vegan food retailers. Or simply turn to page 148 in this book.

Cheese: There are now vegetarian and vegan alternatives for many types of cheese, such as Gouda, Emmental, mozzarella, cream cheese and even Parmesan, which are available from well-stocked organic food shops and online retailers. There can be quite substantial differences in quality, so you'll need to try a few. You'll have to decide for yourself which cheese tastes the best.

Egg: The way to replace egg depends on the recipe. For example, apple purée or ripe bananas can be used to loosen the dough for sweet pastries. For binding mince to make hamburgers, you can use 2 tablespoons of chickpea flour or cornflour instead of one egg. For crumbing, a thick batter, made by mixing flour with water, works well.

Honey: We recommend replacing this with agave syrup or maple syrup.

Yeast flakes: Sooner or later the words 'yeast flakes' will pop up. This name refers to nutritional yeast in flake form. It has an impressively high vitamin B content and is suitable as a condiment to give dishes a cheesy flavour and creamy consistency.

VEGAN TRAFFIC LIGHTS

As a quick and easy guide to which recipes are vegan or veganisable, they are colour-coded using our vegan traffic lights.

This recipe is vegan.

This recipe can be easily veganised.

This recipe is too time consuming to veganise or an entirely new vegan version of this recipe is needed.

TIPS FOR COOKING FAST FOOD

If you haven't got much time to cook, these tips will come in very handy.

1. Keep the kitchen tidy
It's easier to keep track of what you're doing if you have lots of free work surfaces. Cooking is faster and stress-free.

2. Be familiar with the recipe
You should read the recipe through at least once before cooking. This makes it easier to get organised and you avoid making mistakes later on.

3. Have ingredients ready
If you have all the ingredients for the recipe ready before cooking, there will be no need to panic or make mistakes later. You need oil, salt and pepper quite often. So you should keep them near the pot or pan you're using. However, the things you rarely need can be kept in the cupboard, out of the way.

4. Quality equipment
One of the most important things for easy and fast cooking is to have quality cooking equipment. In addition to pots and pans, this should definitely include:
1 large kitchen knife, 1 small kitchen knife, 1–2 large chopping boards, stick blender, food processor, spatula, wooden spoon, whisk, bowls in different sizes, kitchen scales and a kettle.

5. Sharpen knives
Newly sharpened knives cut better. That's why we always recommend sharpening them regularly.

6. Food processor
Ingredients such as onions, carrots and peppers can often be chopped faster and more thoroughly with a food processor or the chopping attachment for your stick blender than with a knife. But be careful not to overdo it, so you aren't left with a vegetable purée.

7. Boil water
You can boil water faster in a kettle than in a pot. Once boiled, simply pour it in.

8. Don't forget the lid
Cooking with a lid keeps the heat in a pot or pan, saving time and energy.

9. Pre-cooked ingredients
Fresh ingredients are naturally preferred as a rule, but when you're in a hurry, using pre-cooked beetroot, for example, can save you a lot of time. You can find a number of pre-cooked ingredients in organic food shops, so at least you are guaranteed the quality of organic produce.

10. Togetherness
According to the adage, too many cooks spoil the broth. But we believe that as long as there's enough room in the kitchen, the work can be perfectly shared between two people.

A FEW MORE THINGS TO CLEAR UP

- We use dried herbs and spices, but you might like to use the fresh variety.

- When a recipe calls for a bunch of herbs, we refer to the small supermarket version of a bunch, not to the large bunches you can find in markets.

- Oven temperatures vary depending on each manufacturer. Always keep an eye on what you've put in the oven and don't put blind faith in our baking times.

- We love garlic, but we use it sparingly. Garlic lovers are welcome to increase the amounts given in the recipes.

- We basically use fresh yeast. If you want to use the dry alternative, replace half a cube of fresh yeast with a sachet of dry yeast.

- Vegetable sizes vary greatly. Unless otherwise stated, use standard size vegetables.

- There are two different types of soy sauce: light and dark (shoyu and tamari for Japanese soy sauce). We only use Japanese tamari soy sauce. This type is produced without the addition of wheat and has a stronger aroma. It is also less salty.

- Leftover dips can also be used as spreads for bread.

- We mainly use olive oil for frying. But this is purely out of habit. If you normally use another kind, such as rapeseed oil, there is no reason for you to change.

SANDWICHES ETC.

Whether spring rolls, pitas or wraps…

… these are eaten without cutlery, although they don't come under the category of burgers or finger food. The variety of dishes presented in the following chapter takes us on a journey through the cuisines of several different countries. From Italy to Mexico, and on to Asia.

TOMATO, ALMOND AND MINT CROSTINI

◆

Crostini aren't only served as starters.
With a side serving of salad, they can easily satisfy two people. The wonderful
freshness of the mint makes this a special taste experience.

INGREDIENTS
Makes about 15
Preparation time: 30 minutes

80 g almonds
250 g cherry tomatoes
50 g sun-dried tomatoes in oil
2 tsp dried mint
1 clove garlic
1 tsp salt
freshly ground pepper
1 baguette
4 tbsp olive oil

Tip
The tomato, almond and mint purée
can also make an excellent sauce
for a serving of pasta.

1. Preheat the oven to 180°C (fan)/gas 6. For the tomato, almond and mint purée, coarsely chop the almonds and toast in a dry frying pan. Wash the cherry tomatoes and combine with the toasted almonds, dried tomatoes, 2 tablespoons of the tomato oil, mint, garlic, salt and pepper in a blender and finely purée.

2. Cut the baguette into fifteen 2½-cm-thick slices. Brush with olive oil and place on a baking tray lined with parchment paper. Bake for 7 minutes in the oven until crispy. Remove from the oven and spread generously with the tomato, almond and mint purée. Return to the oven for 5 more minutes and serve immediately.

APPLE AND ONION CROSTINI

◆

A flavourful orchestration is the best way to describe this combination of sweet apple, slightly sharp onion, aromatic goat's milk Gouda cheese and fragrant thyme.

INGREDIENTS

Makes about 15
Preparation time: 30 minutes

3 red onions
1 clove garlic
7 tbsp olive oil
1 apple
100 g vegetarian Gouda-style cheese
1 tbsp honey
1 tsp dried thyme
salt
freshly ground pepper
1 baguette

1. Preheat the oven to 180°C (fan)/gas 6. For the apple and onion mixture, peel and finely chop the onion and garlic. Heat 3 tablespoons of olive oil in a frying pan. Sweat the garlic and onion over a low heat until translucent. Wash, quarter and core the apple, and then cut into very small dice together with the Gouda. Add together with the honey and thyme to the onions and garlic. Season with salt and pepper.

2. Cut the baguette into fifteen 2½-cm-thick slices. Brush with the remaining olive oil and place on a baking tray lined with parchment paper. Bake for 7 minutes in the oven until crispy. Remove from the oven and spread generously with the apple and onion mixture. Return to the oven for 5 more minutes and serve immediately.

For the vegan version:
The vegan version
leaves out the Gouda cheese.
Replace the honey with 1
teaspoon of agave syrup.

For the vegan version:
use soya yoghurt
instead of plain yoghurt.

CRISPY AVOCADO CHIP BAGEL

◆

Most people enjoy fresh and raw avocado.
For a hearty bagel sandwich, we crumb the avocado flesh with crispy corn flakes
and then bake it in the oven.

INGREDIENTS

Makes 2 bagels
Preparation time: 40 minutes

2 avocados
150 g plain yoghurt
120 g unsweetened corn flakes
salt
freshly ground pepper
chilli flakes
12 cherry tomatoes
½ bunch rocket
2 bagels (see recipe on page 173)
1 serving lemon and cashew mousse (see recipe on page 135)

1. Preheat the oven to 180°C (fan)/gas 6. For the avocado chips, halve the avocados and remove the stone. Slice each half into 4 thick wedges. Stir the yoghurt in a shallow bowl until smooth. Coarsely crush the corn flakes with your hands and put into a second shallow bowl.

2. Coat the avocado wedges with yoghurt on all sides, and then sprinkle with salt, pepper and chilli flakes. Then dredge in the cornflakes and place on a baking tray lined with parchment paper. Bake for 20 minutes in the oven until crispy, turning over halfway through.

3. In the meantime, wash and slice the cherry tomatoes. Wash the rocket and shake dry. Halve the bagels. Generously spread each half with the lemon and cashew mousse. Cover with tomato slices and rocket. Take the avocado chips out of the oven, spread them over the top and serve.

DELUXE TOAST HAWAII

◆

This simple toasted ham, cheese and pineapple open sandwich has been popular worldwide since the 1950s. Leaving out the ham, and with only a little more effort, you can create a version that will impress your guests. As this dish isn't very filling, we recommend it as a starter or a snack.

INGREDIENTS

Makes 4
Preparation time: 30 minutes

50 g vegetarian Parmesan cheese
1 tsp butter
1 tsp wheat flour
150 ml milk
salt
freshly ground pepper
25 g flaked almonds
1 tbsp tamari soy sauce
4 slices tinned pineapple
8 slices toast (see recipe on page 174)
½ bunch chives

◢
Tip
Don't throw away the toast trimmings:
make them into excellent croûtons for a salad
by cooking in a hot frying pan with olive oil, salt,
pepper and Italian herbs. Or eat them as snacks (see
recipe on page 64).

1. Preheat the oven to 180°C (fan)/gas 6. Grate the cheese. Melt the butter in a saucepan and stir in the flour. Add the milk while stirring until smooth, and then bring to the boil. Add the cheese while stirring constantly on a low heat until smooth. Season with salt and pepper, cover with a lid and keep warm.

2. Toast the almonds in a dry frying pan and deglaze with the soy sauce. Drain the pineapple in a sieve. Use a large glass or cup to cut the slices of toast into discs. Toast briefly in a toaster until crispy. Cover the discs with the pineapple slices and toasted almonds. Drizzle with the Parmesan sauce and grill in the oven for about 6 minutes.

3. In the meantime, wash, shake dry and finely chop the chives. Take the grilled toast out of the oven, sprinkle with chives, cover with the remaining toast discs and serve.

ARTICHOKE AND LEMON BUTTER BAGUETTE

◆

Shop-bought herb garlic bread often made a fast and easy meal in our childhood years. From our reminiscences, we revive the herb garlic baguette with this new version that is quick to prepare.

INGREDIENTS

Makes 1
Preparation time: 20 minutes

1 clove garlic
½ untreated lemon
30 g pine nuts
130 g marinated artichoke hearts
2 tbsp chopped parsley
3 tbsp grated vegetarian Parmesan-style cheese
50 ml olive oil
25 g butter
salt
freshly ground pepper
1 baguette

Tip
The artichoke and lemon butter can also be used as a delicious pasta sauce.

1. Preheat the oven to 180°C (fan)/gas 6. For the artichoke and lemon butter, peel and chop the garlic. Rinse the lemon under hot water, squeeze the juice and grate the zest. Toast the pine nuts in a dry frying pan. Combine with the garlic, artichoke hearts, parsley, cheese, olive oil, butter and the lemon juice and zest, and finely purée. Season with salt and pepper.

2. Make cuts in the baguette every 3 cm and use a knife to fill the cuts with a generous amount of the artichoke and lemon butter. Place the baguette on a baking tray lined with parchment paper and bake in the oven for 5–7 minutes until crispy. Serve immediately.

For the vegan version:
Use a plant-based butter substitute. Instead of Parmesan, add more pine nuts and season with yeast flakes.

SAVOURY FRENCH TOAST

◆

This sweet dish is also known as Poor Knight. We felt that it made sense to make a spicy and savoury version, which gave rise to this vegan recipe with a flavour inspired by Asian cuisine.

INGREDIENTS

Makes 8
Preparation time: 40 minutes

100 g chickpea flour
100 g wheat flour
1 tsp ground ginger
1 tsp ground coriander seeds
1 tsp turmeric
2 tsp curry powder
½ yellow pepper
1 small onion

1 small chilli pepper
½ bunch parsley
salt
freshly ground pepper
8 slices toast
  (see recipe on page 174)
8 tbsp olive oil

1. For the batter, combine the chickpea and wheat flours with the spices in a bowl. Add 300 ml of warm water and mix to a smooth batter. Set aside.

2. Wash the pepper. Remove the stalk and seeds, and finely chop. Peel and finely chop the onion. Halve the chilli pepper lengthwise. Remove the stem, seeds and ribs, and finely chop. Wash, shake dry and finely chop the parsley. Mix all the prepared ingredients into the batter and season with salt and pepper.

3. Carefully dip the slices of toast in the batter. You can also use a spoon to spread the batter over them.

4. Preheat the oven to 90°C (fan)/gas ¼. Heat 1 tablespoon of olive oil in a frying pan. Fry a slice of toast on both sides until crispy and brown. Take it out of the pan and keep warm in the oven. Do the same with the rest of the toast.

TUNA-LESS TUNA SANDWICH

◆

*You won't find tuna on our table. But we sometimes still crave the creamy taste
experience that is associated with a tuna sandwich.
Luckily, this can be recreated without the tuna.*

INGREDIENTS

Makes 2
Preparation time: 20 minutes

1 tin chickpeas (drained weight 240 g)
4 tbsp almond mayonnaise (see recipe on page 148)
2 spring onions
2 pickled gherkins
2 tsp fresh dill
2 tsp tamari soy sauce
1 tsp hot pepper and chilli sauce (see recipe on page 139)
salt
freshly ground pepper
6 slices toast (see recipe on page 174)
4 tbsp ketchup
a few iceberg lettuce leaves

1. Drain the chickpeas in a sieve. Combine with the mayonnaise, using a fork or potato masher
to crush into a rough paste. Trim, wash and finely slice the spring onions. Finely dice the gherkins. Add the chopped spring onions and diced gherkins to the chickpea paste and mix well. Fold
in the dill, soy sauce and chilli sauce, and season with salt and pepper.

2. Toast the bread. Spread 4 slices each with 1 tablespoon of ketchup and cover with a few
lettuce leaves. Cover with the chickpea paste. Lay two prepared slices of toast over the other two,
then cover with the remaining slices to make two double-decker tuna-less tuna sandwiches.

Serving tip: Cut the sandwiches on the diagonal with a sharp knife and use a toothpick to hold
them in place. Serve.

MANCHEGO QUESADILLA

WITH BEAN AND CAPER DIP

◆

The quesadilla is a type of Mexican fast food, and its name is a combination of its two main components: cheese (queso in Spanish) and the Mexican tortilla flatbread. We use Spanish Manchego ewe's milk cheese, which can be found at well-stocked supermarket cheese counters. Gouda can be used as an alternative but make sure it is vegetarian, without animal rennet.

INGREDIENTS

Makes 3
Preparation time: 15 minutes

150 g vegetarian Manchego-style cheese
½ bunch chives
6 wheat tortillas (see recipe on page 162)
1 serving bean and caper dip (see recipe on page 136)
oil for frying

1. Grate the cheese. Wash, shake dry and finely chop the chives.

2. Spread the bean and caper dip over 3 tortillas and scatter grated cheese and chopped chives over the top. Cover with the remaining tortillas. Heat some olive oil in a frying pan. Fry each tortilla on both sides until crispy. Cut into quarters and serve.

◢

Tip

For more flavour, use the coriander and mint chutney (see recipe on page 142) as a dip.

FOUR-MUSHROOM WRAP

◆

'Four cheeses' is a bit too run-of-the-mill for us. We make our wrap with four aromatic varieties of mushroom, crispy rocket, spicy goat's milk Gouda and a lovely and refreshing tarragon cream.

INGREDIENTS

Makes 4
Preparation time: 30 minutes

½ bunch spring onions
2 cloves garlic
100 g button mushrooms
100 g shiitake mushrooms
100 g king oyster mushrooms
100 g oyster mushrooms
2 handfuls rocket
50 g goat's milk Gouda cheese or similar vegetarian cheese
2 tbsp olive oil
150 g sour cream
1 tsp dried tarragon
salt
freshly ground pepper
4 wheat tortillas (see recipe on page 162)

1. Trim, wash and finely slice the spring onions. Peel and finely chop the garlic. Clean the mushrooms and cut into large, uniform pieces. Wash the rocket and shake dry. Remove any tough stems. Grate the cheese.

2. Heat the olive oil in a large frying pan. Brown the garlic and mushrooms for 5 minutes over a high heat. Add the spring onions and cook for 2 minutes. Finally, stir in the sour cream and tarragon, and season with salt and pepper.

3. Warm the tortillas for a few minutes in the oven. When they come out, cover with rocket and the mushroom mixture. Sprinkle with grated cheese, roll up and serve.

For the vegan version:

Replace the sour cream with unsweetened soya yoghurt. Instead of Gouda, use a grated vegan cheese, or leave out altogether.

LENTIL DAHL BURRITO

◆

This burrito can be made without too much time and effort.
Red lentils are an excellent source of iron.

INGREDIENTS

Makes 4
Preparation time: 25 minutes

1 onion
1 clove garlic
1 tbsp olive oil
2 tbsp tomato purée
1 tsp ground coriander seeds
½ tsp ground ginger
½ tsp curry powder
½ tsp turmeric
1 tsp chilli powder
150 g red lentils, washed

250 ml coconut milk
400 g tinned chopped tomatoes
1 red chilli pepper
salt
freshly ground pepper
4 wheat tortillas (see recipe on page 162)
a few iceberg lettuce leaves
½ bunch coriander
150 g tinned sweetcorn kernels
200 g sour cream

1. Peel and finely chop the onion and garlic. Heat the olive oil in a small saucepan. Sweat the onion and garlic in the oil. Add the tomato purée and spices and brown together for a few minutes. Add the lentils and mix, then deglaze with the coconut milk and tomatoes.

2. Wash the chilli pepper, remove the seeds and ribs, and cut into small pieces, add it to the saucepan and simmer for 15 minutes over a medium heat, stirring often. Season with salt and pepper.

3. Warm the tortillas in the oven. Wash and shake dry the lettuce and coriander. Drain the sweetcorn in a sieve.

4. Take the tortillas out of the oven and cover with lettuce leaves, sour cream and 4-5 tablespoons of lentil dahl. Scatter sweetcorn and coriander over the top and roll into a burrito.

For the vegan version:
Replace the sour cream with lemon and cashew mousse (see recipe on page 135) or soya yoghurt.

For the vegan version:
Cheddar cheese is delicious,
but it needs to be left out, or
use a vegan cheese.

TORTILLA BOWL SALAD

WITH CORIANDER AND TAHINI DRESSING

◆

This salad is presented in an amusing way, and it surprises with its amazing sesame and coriander dressing.

INGREDIENTS

Makes 4
Preparation time: 45 minutes

4 wheat tortillas (see recipe on page 162)
½ head iceberg lettuce
1 avocado
8 cherry tomatoes
2 spring onions
4 tbsp tinned sweetcorn kernels
4 tbsp tinned kidney beans
40 g vegetarian Cheddar cheese

FOR THE CORIANDER AND TAHINI DRESSING
1 handful coriander
1 lime
½ clove garlic
3 tbsp tahini
2 tsp tamari soy sauce
2 tbsp white wine vinegar
1 tsp tomato purée
salt
freshly ground pepper

1. Preheat the oven to 200°C (fan)/gas 7. To make the tortilla bowls, press the tortillas into small, ovenproof bowls, and then bake in the oven until crispy. A muffin pan can also be used.

2. Separate the lettuce into individual leaves. Wash, shake dry and cut the leaves into strips. Halve the avocado and remove the stone. Scoop the flesh out of the shell and cut into small wedges. Wash and halve the cherry tomatoes. Trim, wash and finely slice the spring onions. Drain the sweetcorn and kidney beans in a sieve.
When the tortilla bowls come out of the oven, leave to cool, then fill with lettuce. Distribute the avocado wedges and cherry tomatoes between the bowls. Scatter the spring onions, sweetcorn and kidney beans over them. Grate cheese over the top.

3. For the coriander and tahini dressing, wash and shake dry the lettuce and coriander. Halve the lime and squeeze the juice. Peel and chop the garlic. Combine with 100 ml of water and the remaining ingredients and purée in a blender. Season with salt and pepper and serve together with the tortilla salad bowls.

MANGO SALSA AND QUINOA WRAP

◆

Quinoa has been used as a staple food in South America for thousands of years. This protein-rich pseudo-cereal is now becoming increasingly popular in this country.

INGREDIENTS
Makes 6
Preparation time: 45 minutes

125 g quinoa
½ lime
1 mango
1 red onion
1 tomato
1 small handful fresh coriander
1 tbsp olive oil

salt
freshly ground pepper
6 wheat tortillas (see recipe on page 162)
150 g crème fraîche
100 g vegetarian feta cheese
4 tbsp milk
½ head iceberg lettuce

1. Prepare the quinoa according to the instructions on the packet. Squeeze the lime. Peel the mango. Remove the flesh from around the stone and cut into small pieces. Peel and finely chop the onion. Wash and dice the tomato. Wash, shake dry and finely chop the coriander. Combine everything with the quinoa, olive oil and lime juice and season with salt and pepper.

2. Warm the tortillas for a few minutes in the oven. Mix the crème fraîche with the feta and milk until smooth. Separate the lettuce leaves, then wash and shake dry. Line the tortillas with a few lettuce leaves. Spread with the feta cream and cover with 2–3 tbsp of the mango salsa and quinoa mixture. Roll them up and serve.

Dip tip: If you want it hot and spicy, you can put some hot pepper and chilli sauce (see recipe on page 139) over the mango sauce.

◢

Tip

The mango salsa with quinoa also makes a great side salad.

For the vegan version:
A vegan mayonnaise
(see recipe on page 148)
is an easy substitute for the
feta cream.

Quinoa

CRISPY CRETE

◆

Feta and olives – an unbeatable duo.
In combination with other Greek salad ingredients they give this amazing
sandwich lots of Mediterranean flair.

INGREDIENTS

Makes 4
Preparation time: 45 minutes

4 eggs
12 tbsp flour
160 g dry breadcrumbs
2 (150 g) pieces vegetarian feta cheese
16 cherry tomatoes
1 yellow pepper
160 g assorted pitted olives
1 serving avocado and garlic dip (see recipe on page 144) or tzatziki
1 bunch chives
6 tbsp olive oil
1 flatbread (see recipe on page 166)
12 butterhead lettuce leaves

1. Beat the eggs with a whisk in a shallow bowl. Prepare the flour and breadcrumbs on separate plates. Cut each piece of feta in half across, and again lengthwise. Dredge each piece in flour, dip in the egg, and then dredge in the breadcrumbs. Set aside the crumbed feta in the refrigerator.

2. In the meantime, wash and halve the cherry tomatoes. Wash the pepper, remove the ribs, stem and seeds, and cut into strips. Finely chop the olives and mix with the avocado and garlic dip or the tzatziki. Wash, shake dry and finely chop the chives.

3. Take the crumbed feta pieces out of the refrigerator. Heat the olive oil in a frying pan, and fry the feta pieces on both sides until golden. Cut the flatbread into quarters. Cut in half through the middle and fill with the lettuce leaves, yellow pepper, feta, cherry tomatoes and chives. Drizzle with the dip or tzatziki and serve.

FALAFEL SANDWICH
WITH RAW VEGETABLE TABBOULEH

◆

This is our version of a falafel sandwich: we fry the chickpea patties in a pan and serve them with tabbouleh and a lime, mint and dill dip (see recipe on page 130)

INGREDIENTS
Makes 4
Preparation time: 30 minutes

FOR THE RAW VEGETABLE TABBOULEH
1 bunch flat-leaf parsley
½ bunch mint
200 g cauliflower florets (about ¼ head)
100 g cherry tomatoes
3 spring onions
½ untreated lemon
3 tbsp olive oil
1 tbsp honey or agave syrup
salt
freshly ground pepper

FOR THE FALAFEL
1 small red onion
1 clove garlic
1 tin chickpeas (drained weight 240 g)
1 tsp harissa paste
1 tsp ground coriander seeds
1 tsp ground ginger
1 tsp cumin
salt
freshly ground pepper
3 tbsp olive oil

OTHERS
4 herb pitas (see recipe on page 164)
a few iceberg lettuce leaves
1 serving lime, mint and dill dip (see recipe on page 130), vegan version

1. For the tabbouleh, wash and shake dry the parsley and mint. Combine with the cauliflower in a blender and chop uniformly. Quarter the tomatoes, and trim, wash and finely slice the spring onions. Rinse the lemon under hot water, squeeze the juice and grate the zest. Mix with the olive oil, honey or agave syrup. Season with salt and pepper.

2. For the falafel patties, peel the onion and garlic. Drain the chickpeas in a sieve. Combine the onions, garlic and chickpeas with the spices in a blender and blend to a smooth paste. Season with salt and pepper, and shape into 8 patties. Heat olive oil in a frying pan. Fry each of the patties over a high temperature on both sides until crispy.

3. For the sandwiches, cut the pitas in half across the middle. Wash and shake dry the lettuce leaves. Fill each of the pitas with lettuce, tabbouleh, two patties and dip, and serve.

Tip

You can use the rest of the cauliflower to make cauliflower slices. Simply cut the cauliflower into slices and boil in salted water, keeping them firm. Crumb the slices and fry until crispy.

CARIBBEAN SPRING ROLLS

◆

Unlike the Chinese spring rolls that are better known in this country, these Vietnamese-style versions use rice paper wrappers instead of ones made from wheat; they are also eaten unfried. This makes them quicker to prepare and without the house smelling of fried food. Great for an evening spent cooking together.

INGREDIENTS

Makes 6
Preparation time: 30 minutes

100 glass (mung bean thread) noodles
½ untreated lemon
1 avocado
1 red pepper
8–10 butterhead lettuce leaves
1 bunch chives
1 handful salted peanuts
6 sheets rice paper (22-cm diameter)
1 serving mango and coconut sauce (see recipe on page 156) or sour cream

1. Prepare the noodles according to the instructions on the packet. Squeeze the lemon. Halve the avocado, remove the seed, scoop the flesh out of the shell and cut into thin slices. Drizzle with lemon juice and set aside.

2. Wash and halve the red pepper, remove the seeds and stem, and finely chop. Wash and shake dry the lettuce and chives. Cut the lettuce into strips and coarsely chop the peanuts.

3. Dip both sides of a sheet of rice paper in lukewarm water for several seconds – it is preferable to fill a large dish or frying pan with water for this purpose. The next step has to be done quickly. Lay the sheet on a flat surface. First lay lettuce and noodles on the wrapper, followed by avocado and red pepper. Drizzle with a generous amount of sauce or sour cream, and sprinkle chopped peanuts over the top. Roll carefully, inserting a few chive leaves into each roll so that the ends stick out, and then serve.

AUTUMN ROLLS

◆

This autumnal version of the spring roll offers the nutty flavour of a wild rice mix combined with spicy Swiss chard and the incomparable beetroot and horseradish dip (see recipe on page 153).

INGREDIENTS

Makes 6
Preparation time: 1 hour

150 g wild rice mix
150 g shiitake mushrooms
2 spring onions
1 bunch Swiss chard
1 tbsp sesame oil
1 tbsp tamari soy sauce

salt
freshly ground pepper
1 small handful raisins
6 sheets rice paper (22-cm diameter)
12 tsp beetroot and horseradish dip (see recipe
   on page 153), vegan version

1. Prepare the rice according to the instructions on the packet. In the meantime, clean and slice the mushrooms. Trim, wash and finely slice the spring onions. Remove the hard stems from the chard, and wash and shake dry. Don't throw away the stems. They can be used in another dish or frozen.

2. Heat the sesame oil in a frying pan. Sear the mushrooms and spring onions for 2 minutes. Deglaze with the soy sauce and season with salt and pepper.

3. Bring a large pot of water to the boil. Blanch the chard leaves for 30 seconds, and then remove and refresh. Drain well. You can also pat the leaves dry with kitchen paper.

4. Mix the raisins with the rice. Dip both sides of a sheet of rice paper in lukewarm water for several seconds – it is preferable to fill a large dish or frying pan with water for this purpose. The next step has to be done quickly. Lay the sheet on a flat surface. Lay 2 tablespoons of rice, 2 teaspoons of beetroot and horseradish dip, the chard and mushrooms on the wrapper. Roll carefully and then serve.

For the vegan version:
Use the vegan version of the
beetroot and horseradish dish.

For the vegan version:
Instead of pecorino cheese, add more breadcrumbs and season with 2 teaspoons of yeast flakes.

OYSTER MUSHROOM SANDWICH

◆

A new interpretation of a classic. Crispy and delicious! Served without the bun, with a garnish and salad, it makes a real treat.

INGREDIENTS
Makes 2
Preparation time: 30 minutes

25 g pine nuts
40 g vegetarian pecorino cheese
40 g dry breadcrumbs
1 tsp rosemary
2 eggs
250 g oyster mushrooms
wheat flour (for dredging)
6 tbsp olive oil
salt
freshly ground pepper
1 handful butterhead lettuce leaves
2 burger buns (see recipe on page 169)
4 tbsp herb and gherkin remoulade (see recipe on page 150)

1. Toast the pine nuts in a dry frying pan. Leave to cool, and then coarsely chop. Finely grate the cheese and mix with the breadcrumbs, rosemary and pine nuts. Beat an egg. Clean the mushrooms, dredge in the flour, dip in the beaten egg, and then dredge in the rosemary crumb coating.

2. Heat the olive oil in a large frying pan. Fry the mushroom for about 3 minutes on both sides until golden brown. Season with salt and pepper.

3. Wash and shake dry the lettuce leaves. Cut the buns in half across the middle. Spread one half of the buns with the herb and gherkin remoulade, then cover with the lettuce leaves and mushrooms. Sandwich with the top half of the bun and serve.

CHANTERELLE PITA

◆

Chanterelle mushrooms are featured here. They are extremely low in fat and
calories, and high in dietary fibre, which makes them deliciously filling.

INGREDIENTS
Makes 4
Preparation time: 30 minutes

300 g chanterelle mushrooms
1 onion
3 tbsp olive oil
2 tbsp gyro spices (see recipe on the right)
salt
freshly ground pepper
1–2 tomato(es)
¼ cucumber
½ bunch flat-leaf parsley
¼ red cabbage
4 herb pitas (see recipe on page 164)
1 serving avocado and garlic dip (see recipe on page 144), vegan version

FOR THE GYRO SPICES
½ tsp curing salt
½ tsp turmeric
2 tsp oregano
1 tsp thyme
½ tsp paprika
¼ tsp rosemary
1 pinch ground cinnamon
1 pinch cumin

1. For the gyro spices, mix all the ingredients together. Clean the mushrooms. Any large ones can be halved or quartered. Peel the onion. Cut in half lengthwise and cut into thin slices.

2. Heat the olive oil in a frying pan. Sear one half of the onion slices and the mushrooms on both sides over a high heat. Add the gyro spices, lower the heat to medium and fry for 8-10 minutes while stirring constantly. Season with salt and pepper.

3. Wash the tomatoes and cucumber, and cut into thin slices. Wash, shake dry and coarsely chop the parsley. Wash the cabbage and cut into strips.

4. Cut the pitas in half across the middle and spread with the avocado and garlic dip. Fill with a little cabbage, mushrooms, parsley, onion, tomato and a few slices of cucumber. Finally, drizzle the rest of the dip over the top and serve.

PICK APART ROLLS

◆

When it comes to eating these bread rolls scored with a chequerboard pattern, there's no need for a knife and fork. Simply pick out each piece and savour each bite.

INGREDIENTS
Makes 4
Preparation time: 30 minutes

1 handful basil
100 ml olive oil
salt
freshly ground pepper
4 bread rolls
100 g vegetarian Emmental-style cheese
80 g pitted black olives
½ yellow pepper
2 tbsp chopped chives

1. Preheat the oven to 180°C (fan)/gas 6. For the basil oil, wash and shake dry the basil leaves. Combine with the olive oil in a blender and purée. Season with salt and pepper.

2. Score the bread rolls every 2½ cm or so across and down. Be careful not to cut through the rolls. Drizzle three-quarters of the basil oil into the cuts.

3. Grate the cheese and chop the olives. Wash the pepper, remove the seeds and finely chop. Fill the cuts in the rolls with cheese, yellow pepper and olives. Sprinkle the chives over the rolls and drizzle with the remaining oil.

4. Bake for 15 minutes and serve immediately.

For the vegan version:
Use vegan cheese.

CHIPS, FINGER FOOD ETC.

If you're tired of the typical chips with salt and vinegar, then this chapter is for you.

Here you will also find small snacks and satisfying finger food which can be prepared as impressive main courses when served with a green salad.

SPICY ROASTED CHICKPEAS

◆

Crisps aren't the only snacks to nibble on while watching a film on television or reading a good book. These easy-to-make roasted chickpeas, can be just as addictive, but without giving you a guilty conscience.

INGREDIENTS
Serves 4
Preparation time: 50 minutes

2 x 400 g tins chickpeas (drained weight each tin 240 g)
2 tbsp olive oil
½ untreated lemon (for grated zest)
1 tsp chilli powder
1 tsp turmeric
1 tsp ground ginger
1 tsp cayenne pepper
1 tsp agave syrup
salt

1. Preheat the oven to 180°C (fan)/gas 6. Drain the chickpeas well in a sieve, and pat dry between two sheets of kitchen paper. Mix with the rest of the ingredients in a bowl and season with salt.

2. Spread the chickpeas out over a baking tray or in a large ovenproof dish. Roast for 40 minutes in the oven, mixing well after 20 minutes. Serve immediately.

◢

Tip

Try these crispy balls in a salad in place of croûtons.

SWEET AND SPICY AUBERGINE STICKS

◆

Not everybody knows that aubergines, strictly speaking, are berries. That they taste good, hopefully, is common knowledge; but just in case, this recipe is meant to set the record straight.

INGREDIENTS

Serves 2
Preparation time: 50 minutes

2 aubergines
1 tsp curry powder
½ tsp chilli flakes
½ tsp ground cinnamon
½ tsp salt
3 tbsp olive oil
2 tbsp maple syrup

1. Preheat the oven to 180°C (fan)/gas 6. Wash and peel the aubergines, and cut into about 1½-cm-thick sticks. Mix with the spices, salt and olive oil in a bowl.

2. Spread out the aubergine sticks over a baking tray or in a large ovenproof dish. Roast in the oven for 20 minutes. Drizzle maple syrup over the aubergine sticks and return to the oven for about 15 minutes more to caramelise. Serve immediately.

Dip tip: We recommend the lime, mint and dill dip (see recipe on page 130).

SPICY CHIPS WITH TOMATO AND CINNAMON

Tomatoey, cinnamony and hot! These make the perfect alternative to conventional chips.

INGREDIENTS

Serves 2
Preparation time: 45 minutes

750 g fast-cooking potatoes
2 tbsp olive oil
1 tbsp tomato purée
1 tsp ground cinnamon
1 tsp cayenne pepper
1 tsp dried basil
salt

Tip

If you associate cinnamon with Christmas and want a different marinade for summer, try making one with olive oil, Italian herbs, lemon juice and grated lemon zest.

1. Preheat the oven to 180°C (fan)/gas 6. Peel the potatoes and cut into 1-cm-thick chips. Soak in a bowl filled with cold water for 10 minutes.

2. For the marinade, combine the olive oil, tomato purée, cinnamon, cayenne pepper and basil and mix well. Drain the chips in a sieve, then carefully mix with the marinade in a bowl.

3. Spread the chips out over a baking tray lined with parchment paper. Bake for 30 minutes in the oven until golden brown, turning them over after 15 minutes. Season with salt before serving.

Dip tip: We recommend almond mayonnaise (see recipe on page 148).

SWEET POTATO PAKORA

◆

Pakora is an Indian dish and consists of one main ingredient. This is dredged in chickpea flour and spices, fried in oil and served as a side dish or snack. Pakora is a particularly popular fast food snack, providing a tasty alternative to chips.

INGREDIENTS

Serves 2
Preparation time: 30 minutes

150 g chickpea flour
1 tsp cayenne pepper
1 tsp turmeric
1 tsp salt
1 tsp nigella seeds
2 spring onions
300 g sweet potatoes
500 ml rapeseed oil

1. Combine the chickpea flour with 170 ml of lukewarm water, the cayenne pepper, turmeric, salt and nigella seeds and mix until smooth. Trim and wash the spring onions, cut lengthwise, chop finely and mix with the batter. Peel the sweet potatoes and cut into 3-mm-thick slices.

2. Heat the rapeseed oil in a deep pan or fryer. Dip the sweet potato in the batter and deep-fry until golden. Drain on kitchen paper and serve.

Dip tip: We recommend serving them with muhammara (see recipe on page 132).

PESTO CROÛTONS

◆

*An unbelievably simple recipe that turns leftover bread and pesto into an
alternative to crisps. And it uses the leftover bread from the chilli and bean rolls
(see recipe on page 76) or deluxe Toast Hawaii (see recipe on page 22).
Of course, you can always use freshly made toast.*

INGREDIENTS
Serves 2
Preparation time: 30 minutes

8 slices toast (see recipe on page 174)
5 tsp pesto alla genovese (see recipe on page 154)
2 tsp white wine vinegar
olive oil

1. Preheat the oven to 180°C (fan)/gas 6. Cut the toast into 2-cm squares and spread out over a
baking tray lined with parchment paper. Bake in the oven for 10 minutes.

2. For the marinade, mix the pesto with the vinegar. You may need to add a little olive oil to
give the marinade more consistency. Take the croûtons out of the oven and carefully mix with
the pesto marinade. Spread out again over the baking tray, return to the oven for another 8-10
minutes and serve immediately.

◢

Tip

These croûtons are also delicious in salads instead
of the usual croûtons.
In this case, cut the bread into small cubes.

For the vegan version:
Use vegan pesto.

For the vegan version:
Replace the cheese with a grated vegan cheese, or leave out altogether.

POTATO WEDGES

WITH A ROSEMARY AND PARMESAN CRUST

◆

The typical seasoning for these potato wedges is made from salt, pepper and paprika. Instead, we use paprika and vegetarian Parmesan cheese. The addition of breadcrumbs makes them particularly crispy. These potato wedges are also known as country-style potatoes.

INGREDIENTS

Serves 2
Preparation time: 45 minutes

500 g fast-cooking potatoes
3 tbsp olive oil
20 g dry breadcrumbs
3 tsp dried rosemary
20 g vegetarian Parmesan cheese
salt
freshly ground pepper

1. Preheat the oven to 180°C (fan)/gas 6. Peel the potatoes, cut into eighths and wash. Pat dry with a cloth and put into a bowl. Add the olive oil, breadcrumbs and rosemary, and grate the cheese over the top. Carefully mix while seasoning with salt and pepper.

2. Spread the potato wedges out over a baking tray lined with parchment paper. Spread any remaining crumb mixture over the cut sides and press firmly. Bake in the oven for 30 minutes until crispy and serve immediately.

Dip tip: We recommend serving them with avocado and garlic dip (see recipe on page 144).

HASSELBACK POTATOES
WITH A LIME, PARMESAN AND DILL TOPPING

◆

This side dish is particularly popular in the US. However, it was invented at the Hasselbacken Restaurant in Stockholm. The Swedish recipe uses perfectly uniform potatoes.

INGREDIENTS
Serves 6
Preparation time: 1 hour

40 g vegetarian pecorino cheese
20 g pine nuts
1 untreated lime
1 clove garlic
½ bunch dill

40 g dry breadcrumbs
8 tbsp olive oil
salt
freshly ground pepper
6 large, fast-cooking potatoes

1. Preheat the oven to 200°C (fan)/gas 7. Finely grate the cheese. Coarsely chop the pine nuts. Rinse the lime under hot water, squeeze the juice and grate the zest. Peel and finely chop the garlic. Wash and shake dry the dill. Separate the tips and chop finely. Mix everything with the breadcrumbs and 4 tablespoons of oil. Season with salt and pepper.

2. Peel the potatoes. Cut off a thin slice from the long side of the potatoes to create a stable base to stop them from rolling. Make slices every 5 mm across the potatoes. An easy way to do this is to lay a chopstick on either side of the potatoes and to cut down until you reach them. You can also use other elongated objects with a width of about 1 cm as a spacer.

3. Rinse the potatoes under running water and carefully bend so that they fan out and as much starch as possible is removed. Pat dry with a cloth. Use a butter knife to spread the filling inside the slits in the potatoes. Spread the potatoes out in a baking dish, drizzle with the remaining oil and bake in the oven for 45 minutes. Take them out of the oven and serve with dill and lime.

Tip

A simple herb butter or our artichoke and lemon butter (see recipe on page 24) can also make a delicious filling. The butter can be left cool and wedges cut and placed inside the slits in the potatoes.

HASSEL BACK

RED RINGS

◆

No fast food cookbook would be complete without onion rings. What we don't want, however, are the typical ones that are dripping with fat. Our impressive baked red rings boast a crisp crumb coating made using beetroot and beer batter and panko, Japanese-style breadcrumbs.

INGREDIENTS

Serves 2
Preparation time: 45 minutes

100 g wheat flour
80 ml milk
80 ml beer
1 tsp mustard
1 tsp salt
1 tsp garlic powder
1 tsp ground ginger
50 g pickled beetroot (from a jar)
100 g panko
300 g red onions

Tip

If you breathe through your mouth when slicing the onions, you can avoid the associated burning sensation in your eyes and resulting tears.

1. Preheat the oven to 220°C (fan)/gas 9. Combine the flour, milk, beer, mustard, salt and spices, and whisk until smooth. Drain the beetroot in a sieve. Grate finely and mix with the batter. Prepare the panko in a separate bowl.

2. Peel the onions, cut into 1-cm-thick slices and separate into rings. Dip each ring into the batter and carefully dredge in the panko.

3. Spread the onion rings out over a baking tray lined with parchment paper. In order to make efficient use of the space, the smaller rings can be placed inside the larger ones. Bake in the oven for 20–25 minutes until crispy and serve immediately.

For the vegan version:
Use vegan milk (see page 10).

For the vegan version:
Replace the cheese with a grated vegan cheese, or leave out altogether.

ASPARAGUS CHIPS

◆

We look forward to asparagus season every year. But we soon find we run out of asparagus recipes. And this is why we've created this exceptional asparagus recipe – wonderfully fresh green asparagus, oven baked with a crispy crumb coating.

INGREDIENTS

Serves 2
Preparation time: 40 minutes

1 bunch green asparagus
3 tbsp olive oil
1 tsp agave syrup
salt
freshly ground pepper
40 g panko
40 g vegetarian Parmesan cheese

1. Preheat the oven to 200°C (fan)/gas 7. Wash the asparagus, peel the lower third of the spears and cut them in half. Remove any woody parts. Mix the asparagus pieces with the olive oil, agave syrup, salt and pepper in a large bowl.

2. Coat the asparagus in the panko in a separate bowl and spread them out over a baking tray lined with parchment paper. Grate the cheese over the asparagus, bake for 20 minutes and serve immediately.

FETA COOKIES

◆

These little things look like chocolate butter biscuits, but they're actually a deliciously addictive savoury snack. Whether you make them as surprise finger food for a party or as a snack is up to you.

INGREDIENTS

Makes about 20
Preparation time: 30 minutes plus resting time

½ untreated lemon
100 g vegetarian feta cheese
30 g cold butter
30 g pitted black olives
1 tsp capers
60 g wheat flour
salt
freshly ground pepper

1. Rinse the lemon under hot water, pat dry and grate the zest. Chop the cheese into small dice and combine with the butter, lemon zest, olives and capers in a food processor and blend to a paste. Add the flour and blend again until smooth. Season with salt and pepper.

2. Knead the dough with your hands over a floured work surface and form into a roll with a diameter of about 5 cm. Wrap in parchment paper and rest for 30 minutes in the refrigerator.

3. Preheat the oven to 180°C (fan)/gas 6. Take the roll out of the refrigerator, remove the paper and use a sharp knife to cut into slices with a thickness of about 2 cm. Spread out over a baking tray lined with parchment paper. Bake in the oven for 20 minutes until golden brown. Serve immediately.

CHILLI AND BEAN ROLLS

◆

Crispy on the outside, creamy on the inside. You can use just about any dip to make these little rolls, but they can only be called chilli and bean rolls if you make them with our chilli and bean dip.

INGREDIENTS
Makes 10
Preparation time: 35 minutes

10 slices toast (see recipe on page 174)
10 tbsp chilli and bean dip (see recipe on page 140)
2 tbsp margarine

1. Cut off the crust from each slice of toast and flatten as much as possible with a rolling pin. Spread 1 tablespoon of chilli and bean dip over each slice of toast. Roll up each slice.

2. Heat the margarine in a large frying pan. Fry each roll on all sides until crispy and brown. Drain on kitchen paper, and then serve.

◢

Tip

Don't throw away the crusts. Use them to make crispy croûtons (see recipe on page 64).

SUSHI ROLLS

◆

Vegetarian sushi is also possible. The trick we used for this is flattened and rolled up toast which, without the need for sticky rice, can quickly conjure up the appearance of delicious sushi rolls on the table.

INGREDIENTS

Makes 40
Preparation time: 35 minutes

1 small courgette
½ bunch chives
10 slices toast (see recipe on page 174)
10 tsp pea hummus (see recipe on page 130)
5 tsp white and black sesame seeds.

1. Wash the courgette, cut off the ends and finely slice. Use a knife to cut the slices into fine strips. Wash, shake dry and finely chop the chives.

2. Cut off the crust from each slice of toast and flatten as much as possible with a rolling pin. Spread each slice of toast with 1 teaspoon of pea hummus. Sprinkle over with courgette strips and chopped chives, roll tightly and press lightly to keep firm. Cut off the untidy ends with a knife, and then cut each roll into four uniform pieces.

3. Put each type of sesame seeds into separate saucers and coat the cut ends of each roll with them. Serve on a plate with the coated surfaces facing upwards.

Tip
These also work well with other dips.
Be creative!

SMUSHI
WITH VEGAN MINCE

◆

A Danish invention, smushi combines traditional smørrebrød with Japanese sushi. The result is finger food with countless possibilities. We top the small open sandwiches with our version of vegan mince. If you can't find puffed rice, crumble up some rice cakes.

INGREDIENTS
Makes 16
Preparation time: 25 minutes

100 ml vegetable broth
2 tbsp tomato purée
1 tbsp ketchup
1 tbsp olive oil
1 tbsp white wine vinegar
1 tsp curry powder
1 tsp agave syrup
50 g puffed rice (from organic food shops)

1 celery stalk
½ onion
1 small tomato
½ bunch flat-leaf parsley
salt
4 slices crispbread
freshly ground pepper
½ punnet cress

1. For the vegan mince, mix the vegetable broth with the tomato purée, ketchup, olive oil, vinegar, curry powder and agave syrup and fold into the puffed rice.

2. Wash and peel the celery stalks. Peel the onion and chop with the celery in a blender or finely dice with a knife. Wash the tomato and finely chop. Wash, shake dry and finely chop the parsley. Mix everything with the rice and season with salt.

3. Carefully cut each slice of crispbread into four pieces with a sharp knife. Top each piece with 1 tablespoon of mince and a little coarsely ground pepper. Decorate with cress and serve.

BURGERS ETC.

It's the best-known fast food, although its origins are a bit of a mystery – we're talking about the burger.

Some claim it comes from the city of Hamburg, while others believe it is an American invention. But one thing is clear: It's loved by practically everybody. Vegetarian versions are more than just spelt patties and wholegrain buns, as you'll see in this chapter.

MUSHROOM AND WALNUT BURGER
WITH RADICCHIO & GORGONZOLA

◆

This autumnal burger livens up the dreary season with its spicy and earthy flavours using different kinds of mushrooms...

INGREDIENTS

Makes 2
Preparation time: 30 minutes

50 g shelled walnuts
1 onion
1 clove garlic
250 g chestnut mushrooms
3 tbsp olive oil
50 g vegetarian Gorgonzola cheese
100 g smetana (sour cream)
1 ripe pear

½ bunch parsley
100 g dry breadcrumbs
1 egg
salt
freshly ground pepper
2 burger buns (see recipe on page 169)
a few radicchio leaves

1. Toast the walnuts in a dry frying pan. Peel and finely chop the onion and garlic. Clean the mushrooms and finely chop in a blender. Heat 2 tablespoons of oil in a frying pan. Sweat the garlic and onion, before adding the chopped mushrooms and browning for 10 minutes. Heat the cheese and smetana in a pan, stirring from time to time.

2. Wash, halve, core and thinly slice the pears. Wash and shake dry the parsley, and then finely chop with the walnuts in a blender. Blend with the mushroom mixture and breadcrumbs and season with salt and pepper. Shape into two large patties. Heat the rest of the oil in a frying pan. Fry the patties on both sides until crispy.

3. Cut the buns in half across the middle and toast for a few minutes under the grill. Wash and shake dry the radicchio leaves. Place one patty, some radicchio and pear slices on the bottom half of each bun and drizzle with Gorgonzola sauce. Cover with the top half and serve.

For the vegan version:

Simply replace the egg (see page 11). Instead of the Gorgonzola sauce, you can also use a vegan garlic sauce (see avocado and garlic dip recipe on page 144).

SQUASH BURGER

◆

An autumnal declaration of love to our homeland.
Here the nutty and savoury flavour of uchiki kuri squash is combined with the
sweet tartness of apple and chestnut purée.
The herb marinade and the highly aromatic notes of the lamb's lettuce tempered
with pumpkin seed oil round out the flavour of these extravagant burgers.

INGREDIENTS

Makes 2
Preparation time: 40 minutes

200 g uchiki (red) kuri squash
1 small apple
2 tbsp olive oil
1 tsp thyme
1 tsp rosemary
2 handfuls lamb's lettuce
2 tbsp pumpkin seed oil
1 tbsp balsamic vinegar
salt
freshly ground pepper
2 burger buns (see recipe on page 169)
sweetened chestnut purée

Tip

If chestnut purée is unavailable, spread the buns
with honey or maple syrup.
You can also make your own chestnut purée. Purée
chestnuts, add milk and cream and reduce, and
sweeten with agave syrup.

1.   Preheat the oven to 160°C (fan)/gas 4. Wash the squash and cut into slices of about 5 mm in thickness. Wash, core and thinly slice the apple. Mix the squash and apple slices with the olive oil, thyme and rosemary. Spread them out over a baking tray lined with parchment paper and bake in the oven for 15 minutes until tender.

2.   In the meantime, thoroughly wash the lamb's lettuce and shake dry. Mix with the pumpkin seed oil and balsamic vinegar. Season with salt and pepper.

3.   Cut the buns in half across the middle and warm for a few minutes in the oven. Spread the bottom half of each bun with 1 tablespoon of chestnut purée and then cover with squash and apple slices and lamb's lettuce. Cover with the top half and serve.

For the vegan version:
Leave out the cheese and use
our vegan mayonnaise.
Replace the egg as explained
on page 11.

Tip

Use the leftover lamb's lettuce to prepare a delicious
side salad. Simply mix 4 tablespoons of walnut oil,
1 tablespoon of raspberry vinegar, 1 teaspoon of
sweet mustard, salt and pepper to make a dressing
and drizzle over the lettuce.

ALPINE VEGGIE BURGER

◆

It might seem strange at first to fill a lye roll with a bread dumpling, but once you've tried it, you won't need convincing to want to try it again.

INGREDIENTS
Makes 2
Preparation time: 1 hour

150 g (about 2) day-old Bavarian pretzels
80 ml lukewarm milk
1 small onion
1 bunch flat-leaf parsley
50 g vegetarian Gruyère-style cheese
6 radishes
120 g coleslaw
6 tsp sweet mustard

6 tsp smetana (sour cream)
2 handfuls lamb's lettuce
1 egg
salt
freshly ground pepper
freshly ground nutmeg
2 tbsp olive oil
2 lye rolls (see recipe on page 170)

1. Chop up the pretzel into small pieces and soak in the milk for 20 minutes. Stir repeatedly, mashing up the pretzel pieces. It should form a sticky paste.

2. Peel and finely chop the onion. Wash, shake dry and finely chop the parsley. Grate the cheese. Trim, wash and finely slice the radishes. Drain the coleslaw in a sieve. Mix the mustard with the smetana. Wash and shake dry the lamb's lettuce.

3. Mix the onion, parsley, cheese and egg with the pretzel paste. Season with salt, pepper and a pinch of nutmeg. If the pretzels are highly salted, you may not need to add any more salt. Shape the paste into two patties.

4. Heat the oil in a frying pan. Sear the patties well on both sides, cover with a lid and leave to cook on a low heat for 5 minutes. Cut the lye rolls in half across the middle. Spread both halves with the mustard and smetana mixture and cover the bottom half of each roll with lamb's lettuce, coleslaw, radish and a patty. Cover with the top half and serve.

PAKORA BURGER

A special kind of multiculturalism: Indian pakora crossed with the epitome of American food culture.

INGREDIENTS

Makes 2
Preparation time: 30 minutes

100 g fast-cooking potatoes
100 g broccoli
80 g chickpea flour
1 tsp turmeric
1 tsp chilli powder
½ tsp cumin
salt
freshly ground pepper
2 tbsp olive oil
4 Chinese cabbage leaves
½ bunch flat-leaf parsley
2 burger buns (see recipe on page 169)
4 tbsp peanut and ginger dip (see recipe on page 142)

Tip

If you don't feel like making the peanut and ginger dip, you can add a little ginger to the patty mixture and spread the burger buns with peanut butter.

1. Peel the potatoes and grate into a bowl. Wash the broccoli, chop in a food processor and mix with the potatoes. Mix the chickpea flour and spices with 100 ml of lukewarm water. Season with salt and pepper. Stir the potato and broccoli into the batter. Shape the paste into two patties.

2. Heat the olive oil in a frying pan, and fry the patties on both sides until golden. Wash and shake dry the Chinese cabbage and the parsley. Cut the Chinese cabbage into strips and remove the stems from the parsley.

3. Cut the buns in half across the middle and spread 1 tablespoon of peanut and ginger dip on the inside of both halves. Cover the bottom half of each bun with a small handful of Chinese cabbage strips and parsley. Place the pakora patties on top, cover with the top half of the buns and serve.

RICOTTA BALL BURGER

◆

Sweet ricotta, spicy Parmesan, aromatic pesto and our unbeatable tomato and pepper relish (see recipe on page 147): the United Flavours of Italy.

INGREDIENTS

Makes 2
Preparation time: 20 minutes

30 g vegetarian Parmesan cheese
150 g vegetarian ricotta cheese
25 g dry breadcrumbs
salt
freshly ground pepper
2 tbsp olive oil
4 butterhead lettuce leaves
2 burger buns (see recipe on page 169)
4 tbsp rocket and pistachio pesto (see recipe
    on page 153) or a green pesto
4 tbsp tomato and pepper relish (see recipe on
    page 147) or tomato sauce

1. Grate the Parmesan and knead together with the ricotta and breadcrumbs. Season with salt and pepper, and shape into 8 reasonably large balls. Heat the olive oil in a frying pan, and fry the patties on all sides until brown.

2. In the meantime, wash the lettuce and shake dry. Cut the buns in half across the middle and spread the cut sides of all the buns with the rocket and pistachio pesto. Place a lettuce leaf and 4 ricotta balls on the bottom half of each bun. Cover with the tomato and pepper relish and another lettuce leaf, then with the top of the bun and serve.

CARROT DOG

◆

You don't need meat, tofu or seitan to make a delicious hot dog.
This recipe is proof.

INGREDIENTS

Makes 4
Preparation time: 25 minutes

4 carrots (the length and thickness of a sausage)
salt
freshly ground pepper
½ cucumber
200 g sauerkraut
1 serving fried onions (see recipe on the right)
4 hot dog buns
1 serving mustard and apricot dip (see recipe on page 144)

FOR THE FRIED ONIONS
2 onions
2 tbsp margarine
salt
freshly ground pepper
2 tbsp wheat flour

1. Peel, top and tail the carrots. Cover with water in a pan, add salt and bring to the boil. Cover with the lid and simmer for 8 minutes. The cooking time may vary depending on the thickness of the carrots. They shouldn't become too soft, and they shouldn't be too hard either, naturally. Refresh the carrots in cold water, drain in a colander and season with pepper.

2. In the meantime, wash the cucumber and cut into fine spirals with a spiralizer, if available; otherwise, cut into fine strips. Drain the sauerkraut well in a sieve.

3. For the fried onions, peel, halve and slice the onions into half-rings. Heat the margarine in a frying pan, add the onions, sweat for a few minutes and season with salt and pepper. Dredge in the flour and fry until crispy, stirring constantly.

4. Cut the buns open lengthwise and spread the cut sides with the mustard and apricot dip. Place the carrot first, and then add the cucumber and sauerkraut. Add a generous amount of fried onions and serve.

For the vegan version:
Replace the egg as explained on page 11. Replace the buffalo mozzarella with a vegan mozzarella.

ITALY-FV

◆

This is a great recipe when you need something fast and easy. Take frozen vegetables, bind with egg (or substitute) and breadcrumbs, and add appropriately themed garnishes to your burger.

INGREDIENTS
Makes 2
Preparation time: 30 minutes

200 g frozen Italian vegetables (courgette, green beans, broccoli, peppers, broad beans etc.)
1 egg
50 g dry breadcrumbs
salt
freshly ground pepper
2 tbsp olive oil
1 ball vegetarian mozzarella cheese
1 handful basil leaves
2 burger buns (see recipe on page 169)
4 tbsp tomato and pepper relish (see recipe on page 147) or tomato sauce

1. Prepare the frozen vegetables according to the instructions on the packet, then coarsely mash with a stick blender. Incorporate the egg and breadcrumbs, season with salt and pepper and shape the paste into two patties. Heat the olive oil in a frying pan, and fry the patties on both sides until crispy.

2. Drain the mozzarella in a sieve, and then cut into slices. Wash the basil leaves and shake dry. Cut the buns in half across the middle. Cover the bottom half of each bun with tomato and pepper relish, a patty, buffalo mozzarella and basil leaves. Cover with the top half and serve.

TEX-MEX BURGER

◆

Tex-Mex cuisine combines the cooking style of the American southern states with Mexican cuisine. This burger is a good example of this.

INGREDIENTS

Makes 4
Preparation time: 45 minutes

½ onion
2 cloves garlic
½ pepper
1 small red chilli pepper
1 celery stalk
1 tin kidney beans (drained weight 240 g)
1 egg
50 g dry breadcrumbs
salt
freshly ground pepper

1 avocado
½ untreated lemon
½ pre-cooked corn on the cob
1 tbsp olive oil
4 large iceberg lettuce leaves
50 g vegetarian Manchego-style cheese
4 burger buns (see recipe on page 169)
4 tbsp almond mayonnaise (see recipe on page 148) or ordinary mayonnaise

1.   Preheat the oven to 200°C (fan)/gas 7. Peel the onion and garlic. Wash and de-seed the pepper and chilli. Wash and peel the celery. Coarsely chop everything first, and then finely chop in a blender.

2.   Tip the beans into a sieve and drain well. Transfer to a bowl and mash with a fork. Add the chopped vegetables, egg and breadcrumbs and knead into a dough. Season with salt and pepper, and shape into 4 patties. Place on a greased baking tray and bake in the oven for 10 minutes.

3.   For the avocado cream, halve the avocado, remove the stone and scoop out the flesh. Squeeze the lemon. Combine the ingredients and mash. Season with salt and pepper. Turn the patties over once and return to the oven for another 10 minutes.

4.   Remove the sweetcorn kernels from the cob by slicing down the cob with a kitchen knife. Heat the oil in a frying pan and brown the sweetcorn. Wash and shake dry the lettuce leaves. Grate the cheese.

5.   Cut the buns in half across the middle. Spread the bottom half of each bun with the avocado cream, and then cover with a lettuce leaf. Spread the top half of each bun with mayonnaise. Sprinkle the patties with grated cheese and return to the oven for 5 minutes to melt the cheese. Take out of the oven and place on the bottom half of the buns. Top with sweetcorn, cover with the top half of the buns and serve.

For the vegan version:
Replace the egg as explained on page 11. Replace the cheese with a vegan cheese, or leave out altogether.

For the vegan version:
A tasty alternative to halloumi cheese is a thin slice of smoked tofu.

EXOTIC DREAM

◆

Perfect for summer! Perfect for a barbecue! All the ingredients can be prepared without any trouble on the grill.

INGREDIENTS

Makes 2
Preparation time: 45 minutes

1 ripe mango
1 bunch spring onions
6 tbsp ketchup
2 tbsp dark balsamic vinegar
hot pepper and chilli sauce
   (see recipe on page 139)
   or chilli sauce, according to preference
1 handful basil leaves
250 g vegetarian halloumi cheese
3 tbsp olive oil
2 herb pitas (see recipe on page 164)

1. Peel the mango, remove the stone and cut into thin wedges. Wash the spring onions. Remove the dark green part and any roots. Cut into lengths of about 7 cm and set aside. Mix the ketchup with the balsamic vinegar and hot pepper and chilli sauce. Wash the basil leaves and shake dry. Cut the halloumi into 1½-cm-wide strips.

2. Heat 1 tablespoon of olive oil in a frying pan and soften the spring onions over a medium heat while stirring constantly. Heat the remaining olive oil in another frying pan, and fry the halloumi slices on both sides until golden brown.

3. Cut the pitas in half across the middle and spread with the ketchup and balsamic vinegar sauce. Over the bottom half of the pitas, alternate the spring onion, halloumi, mango and basil leaves. Cover with the top and serve.

PRINCESS IRONHEART

◆

The name of this burger comes from the sweet flavour and the high iron content of amaranth. For anybody who wants to offer something different for breakfast or brunch, or to have with coffee or as a dessert.

INGREDIENTS

Makes 2
Preparation time: 1 hour

60 ml milk
70 g amaranth
2 tbsp rolled oats
½ untreated lemon
3 cm vanilla pod
1-2 clove(s)
1 pinch ground cinnamon
1 tsp raw cane sugar
2 ripe peaches

4 mint leaves
1 egg
3 tbsp dry breadcrumbs
1 tbsp rapeseed oil
2 burger buns (see recipe on page 169)
4 tbsp stewed apple (from a jar)

1. Combine the milk, amaranth, oats and 100 ml of water in a pan and bring to the boil. Rinse the lemon under hot water, grate the zest, add to the porridge and mix. Split the vanilla pod, scrape out the seeds, add to the porridge with the cloves, cinnamon and sugar and mix. Leave to simmer for 30 minutes, stirring from time to time, and add liquid if necessary. Remove the vanilla pod and the cloves, and allow the porridge to cool down.

2. Wash, core and slice the peaches. Wash the mint, shake dry and cut into strips. Mix the egg and breadcrumbs into the porridge.

3. Heat rapeseed oil in a frying pan. Use two tablespoons to shape the porridge into 2 patties and place in the pan. Fry on both sides until crispy. Leave to cook on a low heat for about 5 minutes.

4. Cut the buns in half across the middle. Cover the bottom of each bun with peach slices, a patty, a dab of stewed apple and mint. Cover with the top half and serve.

For the vegan version:

Use a vegan alternative to milk and replace the egg as explained on page 11.

BITTER-SWEET TEMPEH

◆

Tempeh is the wonder protein of vegan cooking.
With a protein content of about twenty per cent and a special, incomparable
flavour, its place is ensured in our cookbook.

INGREDIENTS

Makes 2
Preparation time: 15 minutes plus marinating time

1 lime
5 tbsp tamari soy sauce
3 tbsp maple syrup
1 tsp harissa paste
1 tsp ground coriander seeds
50 ml vegetable broth
200 g tempeh (roll)
1 grapefruit

3 tsp tahini
1 tbsp agave syrup
2 tbsp white balsamic vinegar
oil for frying
2 burger buns (see recipe on page 169)
2 handfuls mild sprouts
   (e.g. alfalfa or mung bean sprouts)

1. For the marinade, squeeze the lime and mix the juice with the soy sauce, maple syrup, harissa, coriander and vegetable broth. Cut the tempeh into 1½-cm-thick slices and marinate for 1 hour.

2. In the meantime, peel and supreme the grapefruit. For the sauce, mix the tahini with the agave syrup, balsamic vinegar and a little water.

3. Heat some oil in a frying pan. Fry the tempeh slices for 2 minutes on both sides. Drizzle the marinade over the tempeh a spoonful at a time. Add a little more maple syrup and leave for a few minutes to caramelise.

4. Cut the buns in half across the middle. Spread each of the halves with 1 tablespoon of sauce. Cover the bottom half of each bun with tempeh and grapefruit segments. Make a nest of shoots on top and drizzle with sauce. Cover with the top half and serve.

For the vegan version:
Use soya or oat cream.
Use yeast flakes instead of
Parmesan, and replace the
egg as explained on page 11.
Sprinkle with vegan cheese.

Tip
These bean balls naturally taste great with
spaghetti and tomato sauce, or plain with chips.

BEAN BALL BURGER

◆

*Owing to their nutritional value, pulses are known in Italy as 'poor man's meat'.
We use haricot beans to create a spicy equivalent of meatballs, and combine
them with a hot pepper sauce for a very special burger, modelled on the popular
meatball sandwich.*

INGREDIENTS

Makes 4
Preparation time: 40 minutes

FOR THE SAUCE
2 onions
2 tbsp olive oil
1 heaped tbsp wheat flour
100 ml vegetable broth
200 ml whipping cream
3 tbsp ajvar (roasted red pepper
    and aubergine relish)
2 tbsp medium-strength mustard
salt
freshly ground pepper

OTHERS
4 burger buns (see recipe on page 169)

FOR THE BEAN BALLS
250 g tinned haricot beans
40 g sun-dried tomatoes
1 clove garlic
20 g vegetarian Parmesan cheese, more for
    sprinkling
40 g dry breadcrumbs
1 egg
1 tsp dried oregano
1 tsp dried basil
salt
freshly ground pepper
2 tbsp olive oil

1. For the sauce, peel and finely chop the onions. Heat the oil in a pan and sweat the onions until translucent. Fold in the flour and deglaze with the broth and cream. Incorporate the ajvar and mustard, bring to the boil for a few minutes, then season with salt and pepper. Leave to simmer gently for 20 minutes.

2. Preheat the oven to 100°C (fan)/ gas ½. For the bean balls, drain the beans in a sieve and finely purée in a blender. Drain the tomatoes in a sieve. Peel the garlic, combine with the tomatoes and finely chop. Grate the cheese. Mix everything with the breadcrumbs, egg and herbs. Season with salt and pepper.

3. Use you hands to shape the bean paste into balls with a diameter of about 2½ cm. Heat the oil in a frying pan and fry the balls one at a time on all sides until brown and crispy, turning over carefully. Keep warm in the oven.

4. Cut the buns in half across the middle. Cover the bottom half of each bun with the bean balls and pepper and cream sauce, and then sprinkle with grated cheese. Cover with the top half and serve.

PIZZA ETC.

Tarte flambée, lahmacun, pizza – topped or filled flatbread have become an integral part of international cuisine.

This chapter shows how it's possible to go beyond the conventional toppings and varieties. By the way, Saturday is said to be the day when most pizza is eaten around the world.

BROCCOLI NAAN

◆

The word naan comes from the Persian word for 'bread'. We fill it with broccoli and spicy diced onion. Best enjoyed warm with dip or it can be eaten cold on the go.

INGREDIENTS
Makes 4
Preparation time: 1 hour

50 g shelled walnuts
1 onion
1 clove garlic
170 g broccoli florets
salt
freshly ground pepper
1 serving all-purpose dough (see recipe on page 161)
4 tbsp olive oil
2 tsp nigella seeds

1.   Preheat the oven to 90°C (fan)/gas ¼. For the broccoli paste, coarsely chop the walnuts and toast in a dry frying pan. Peel the onion and garlic. Wash and carefully pat dry the broccoli, and finely blend together with the walnuts, onion and garlic. Season with salt and pepper.

2.   Divide the dough into four uniform pieces. Roll each piece out thinly and spread the broccoli paste over them. Fold up the sides, squeeze together, turn the dough over and roll out again.

3.   Lay the naans on 2 baking trays lined with parchment paper, brush each one with 1 table-spoon of olive oil and sprinkle with nigella seeds. Turn off the oven, and then put the trays into the oven for 20 minutes. Set the oven temperature to 220°C (fan)/gas 9. Bake for 15 minutes and serve immediately.

Dip tip: We recommend the lime, mint and dill dip (see recipe on page 130).

TARTE FLAMBÉE
WITH CAMEMBERT AND APRICOTS

◆

Fancy a holiday in France?
Unfortunately, we aren't able to provide that service. But this recipe offers you a
flavour that's as good as being there.

INGREDIENTS
Makes 1
Preparation time: 45 minutes

1 serving all-purpose dough (see recipe on page 161)
200 g vegetarian Camembert-style cheese
5 ripe apricots
30 g shelled walnuts
100 g crème fraîche
salt
freshly ground pepper
1 tsp rosemary

1. Preheat the oven to 90°C (fan)/gas ¼. Roll the dough out thinly, turn up the edges a little and lay it on a baking tray lined with parchment paper. Turn off the oven, and then put the tray into the oven for 20 minutes.

2. Cut the cheese into strips. Wash and halve the apricots, remove the stones and cut into wedges. Coarsely chop the walnuts.

3. Take the tray out of the oven. Preheat the oven to 220°C (fan)/gas 9. Cover the dough with crème fraîche. Season with salt and pepper, and sprinkle with rosemary. Evenly distribute the cheese and apricots over the top. Scatter the walnuts over the top, and then bake in the oven for 8 minutes. Serve immediately.

TARTE FLAMBÉE

WITH CASHEW & OLIVE TAPENADE AND ARTICHOKE HEARTS

◆

This recipe proves that a tarte flambée works without the requisite crème fraîche. Soaked and finely puréed cashew nuts give it a creamy consistency, while olives and artichoke hearts add an incomparably aromatic flavour.

INGREDIENTS

Makes 1
Preparation time: 15 minutes plus soaking time

50 g cashew nuts
1 serving all-purpose dough (see recipe on page 161)
75 g pitted green olives
75 g pitted black olives
3 tbsp olive oil
250 g marinated artichoke hearts
1 onion
salt
freshly ground pepper

Tip

If you can't bear to go without cheese, you can make this dish with vegetarian cheese.

1. Soak the cashews in 50 ml of water for 2 hours. Preheat the oven to 90°C (fan)/gas ¼. Roll the dough out thinly, turn up the edges a little and lay on a baking tray lined with parchment paper. Turn off the oven, and then put the tray into the oven for 20 minutes.

2. Drain the olives in a sieve. Combine with the olive oil and cashews and their soaking water in a blender and finely purée. Drain the artichoke hearts in a sieve. Peel the onion. Cut in half lengthwise and cut into thin slices.

3. Take the tray out of the oven. Preheat the oven to 220°C (fan)/gas 9. Cover the dough with the cashew and olive tapenade and spread the onions and artichoke hearts evenly over the top. Bake in the oven for 9 minutes, season with salt and pepper, and serve immediately.

PIZZA BIANCA MANDARINO E PISTACCHIO

◆

A pizza you are guaranteed to never have tried. Instead of the usual toppings, this baked treat combines sweet-and-sour mandarin with the aromatic flavour of pistachio.

INGREDIENTS

Makes 2
Preparation time: 45 minutes

1 serving all-purpose dough (see recipe on page 161)
1 small red onion
250 g vegetarian mozzarella cheese
1 tin unsweetened mandarin wedges (drained weight 175 g)
2 tsp dried oregano
1 handful chopped pistachio nuts
salt
freshly ground pepper

1. Preheat the oven to 90°C (fan)/gas ¼. Halve the dough ball, roll out into two even discs and place each pizza base on a separate baking tray lined with parchment paper. Turn off the oven, and then put the trays into the oven for 20 minutes.

2. Peel the onion and cut into thin slices. Drain the mozzarella in a sieve, and then cut into thin slices. Drain the mandarin wedges in a sieve.

3. Take the pizza bases out of the oven. Preheat the oven to 220°C (fan)/gas 9. Spread the mozzarella slices evenly over the pizza bases. Spread the onion and mandarin wedges over the top, sprinkle with oregano and then bake in the oven for 15 minutes. Halfway through baking, scatter the chopped pistachios over the pizzas.

4. Take the pizzas out of the oven, season with salt and pepper, and serve immediately.

For the vegan version:
Replace the ricotta with lemon and cashew mousse (see recipe on page 135).

AUBERGINE AND RICOTTA POCKETS

◆

Hot or cold, these filled pockets are always a treat.

INGREDIENTS
Makes 4
Preparation time: 1 hour

1 serving all-purpose dough
  (see recipe on page 161)
2 aubergines
salt
1 onion
1 clove garlic
4 tbsp olive oil
2 tsp harissa paste

1 tbsp tomato purée
1 small handful basil leaves
1 tbsp mint leaves
1 tbsp flat parsley leaves
100 g vegetarian ricotta cheese
freshly ground pepper
1 tsp coarse sea salt

1. Divide the dough into four pieces and roll each one out into an oval. Lay the pieces on 2 baking trays lined with parchment paper and leave in a warm place. Preheat the oven to 220°C (fan)/gas 9. Wash and dice the aubergines, and then mix with 2 teaspoons of salt in a sieve. Peel and finely chop the onion and garlic.

2. Heat 2 tablespoons of oil in a pan. Sweat the onion and garlic. Fry the harissa with the tomato purée. Add the aubergines and fry for 2 minutes while stirring constantly. Cook on a low heat for 30 minutes, stirring from time to time.

3. Wash and shake dry the basil, mint and parsley leaves. Coarsely purée together with the aubergine mixture. Incorporate the cheese and season with salt and pepper. Spread the mixture over the centre of the dough ovals. Position the ovals with the short side towards you, and then fold up the long side. Brush with the rest of the oil and sprinkle over with sea salt. Bake for 15 minutes until golden brown, and serve immediately.

◢
Tip
Any leftover filling will make an excellent sauce for
a serving of pasta.

PITA MARGHERITA

◆

The archetype pizza with a twist.
Its name is attributed to Queen Margherita of Italy, who had pizza brought
to her palace. We also believe that she was responsible for the invention of the
pizza delivery service.

INGREDIENTS

Makes 6
Preparation time: 30 minutes

125 g vegetarian mozzarella cheese
8–10 cherry tomatoes
3 herb pitas (see recipe on page 164)
6 tbsp blizza sauce (see recipe on page 136)
20 g pine nuts
1 clove garlic
1 bunch basil
50 ml olive oil
20 g vegetarian Parmesan cheese
salt
freshly ground pepper

1. Preheat the oven to 220°C (fan)/gas 9. Drain the mozzarella in a sieve, and then tear into small pieces. Wash and slice the tomatoes. Cut the pitas in half through the middle and lay with their cut side facing upwards on a baking tray. Cover each half with 1 tablespoon of blizza sauce. Arrange the tomato slices, mozzarella pieces and pine nuts over the top and bake in the oven for 8 minutes.

2. For the pesto, peel the garlic. Wash the basil, shake dry and pluck the leaves. Combine with the garlic and olive oil in a blender and purée to a fine paste.

3. Take the pita margheritas out of the oven. Drizzle with pesto and grate Parmesan over the top. Season with salt and pepper, and serve.

PITA

MARGHERITA

VEGGIE LAHMACUN

◆

Lahmacun means 'meat with dough'. We think this needn't be the case, and we show that it also works without meat and, more particularly, that it tastes good. It's quick to make with our yeast-free recipe for wheat tortillas. Of course, it would be faster if you use store-bought ones.

INGREDIENTS
Makes 6
Preparation time: 45 minutes

1 red pepper
½ green pepper
2 green chilli peppers
1 onion
1 clove garlic
2 tomatoes
1 handful flat-leaf parsley
80 g cashew nuts

2 tbsp tomato purée
1 tsp paprika
3 tbsp olive oil
salt
freshly ground pepper
6 wheat tortillas (see recipe on page 162)
1 small head iceberg lettuce

1. Preheat the oven to 220°C (fan)/gas 9. Wash the peppers and chillies and remove the seeds, ribs and stems. Peel the onion and garlic. Wash the tomatoes and coarsely chop together with the peppers, onion and garlic into small pieces. Wash the parsley, shake dry and pluck off a handful of leaves. Combine everything with the cashews, tomato purée, paprika and olive oil in a blender and blend to a coarse sauce. Season with salt and pepper.

2. Cover the tortillas with the sauce and bake in the oven for 5–8 minutes. Wash the lettuce and cut the leaves into strips. Cover the tortillas with lettuce and roll them up to eat with your hands.

Tip

Don't pre-bake homemade tortillas.

PIZZA POTATOES

◆

Chips or pizza? Can't decide?
Then try our pizza potatoes.

INGREDIENTS
Makes 2 trays
Preparation time: 40 minutes

400 g large, fast-cooking potatoes
2 tbsp olive oil
80 g vegetarian Emmental-style cheese
1 serving blizza sauce (see recipe on page 136)

1. Preheat the oven to 180°C (fan)/gas 6. Wash and peel the potatoes, and cut into slices about 3 mm thick. Mix well with the olive oil in a bowl. Lay the slices over two baking trays lined with parchment paper, without overlapping. Bake in the oven for 15 minutes. In the meantime, grate the cheese.

2. Take the trays out of the oven. Cover the potato slices with blizza sauce and scatter the cheese over the top. Return to the oven for another 12 minutes to melt the cheese. Serve immediately.

◢

Tip

Large potatoes are easier to use than smaller ones.

For the vegan version:
Replace the Emmental with a grated vegan cheese, or leave out altogether.

For the vegan version:
Replace the goat's cheese with a vegan cream cheese or a vegan spread.

LIMO

LEEK AND GOAT'S CHEESE MINI PIZZAS

◆

Size isn't everything. Our leek and goat's cheese mini pizzas are proof of this.
Their handy size ensures that every bit is even more enjoyable.

INGREDIENTS
Makes 10
Preparation time: 40 minutes

1 serving all-purpose dough (see recipe on page 161)
2 leeks
2 onions
2 cloves garlic
150 g vegetarian goat's cheese
1 tbsp olive oil
2 tbsp dried cranberries
4 tsp dried tarragon
salt
freshly ground pepper

1. Preheat the oven to 90°C (fan)/gas ¼. Divide the dough into ten uniform pieces and roll them out thinly into discs. Spread out over two baking trays lined with parchment paper. Turn off the oven, and then put the trays into the oven for 20 minutes.

2. In the meantime, wash the leeks and cut into rings. Peel and finely chop the onions and garlic. Cut the cheese into large chunks.

3. Heat the olive oil in a frying pan and sweat the onions and garlic. Add the leeks and sweat for about 5 minutes while stirring constantly. Incorporate the cheese and cranberries. Season with tarragon, salt and pepper.

4. Preheat the oven to 220°C (fan)/gas 9. Cover the pizza bases with a generous amount of the leek and cheese mixture. Bake in the oven for 7 minutes until crispy and serve immediately.

DIPS, SAUCES ETC.

Fast food's secret heroes…

…at times, subtle and sweet in the background, and at others, brash and fiery in the limelight. Without dips, sauces and spreads, so many burgers would be dry and the taste experience would be too one-sided. The classics are ketchup and mayonnaise. But without wanting to be complacent, we offer you a copious number of recipes and ideas for irresistible alternatives.

LIME, MINT AND DILL DIP

◆

With the freshness of lime and mint, the fragrant zestiness of dill and the sweet acidity of yoghurt, this dip targets many of your taste buds. It goes well with many dishes, but is a standout with a baguette loaf.

INGREDIENTS

Makes 300 g
Preparation time: 10 minutes

½ bunch mint
½ bunch dill
2 untreated limes
300 g plain yoghurt
1 tsp honey or agave syrup
salt
white pepper

Wash, shake dry and finely chop the mint and dill. Rinse the limes under hot water, pat dry and grate the zest. Combine 2 tablespoons of lime juice with all the ingredients and mix until smooth. Season with salt and pepper. It can keep in the refrigerator for about 1 week.

PEA HUMMUS

◆

There are lots of recipes for chickpea hummus. We offer a version made with peas, which is characterised by its special freshness.

INGREDIENTS

Makes 250 g
Preparation time: 15 minutes

200 g frozen peas
1 clove garlic
½ untreated lemon
1 tbsp tahini
1 tbsp smetana (sour cream)
¼ tsp cumin
¼ tsp ground coriander seeds
salt
freshly ground pepper
2 tbsp olive oil

Boil the peas in 100 ml of water for 3 minutes with the lid on, then strain. Peel and chop the garlic. Rinse the lemon under hot water, squeeze the juice and grate the zest. Combine the garlic, lemon juice and zest, peas and other ingredients and finely purée. Season with salt and pepper, and drizzle with olive oil. Serve. It can keep in the refrigerator for about 1 week.

For the vegan version:
Use soya yoghurt.

For the vegan version:
The smetana makes the
hummus smooth and creamy.
Replace with soya yoghurt or
leave out.

FLASH MUHAMMARA

This paste is originally from Syria and can serve as a dip for so many dishes. Made with roasted peppers from a jar, this muhammara is quick to prepare and makes an interesting change from Marie Rose, garlic or BBQ sauce at any barbecue.

INGREDIENTS

Makes 350 g
Preparation time: 15 minutes

1 jar roasted peppers (drained weight 270 g)
1 clove garlic
40 g shelled walnuts
2 tbsp dry breadcrumbs
½ tsp cumin
½ tsp ground cinnamon
2 tsp honey or agave syrup
2 tsp red curry paste
1 tbsp tomato purée
50 ml olive oil
salt
freshly ground pepper

Tip

We use roasted peppers from a jar because it's quicker. Of course you can always roast them yourself. To do this, simply quarter two red peppers and place under the oven grill until the skin blisters and turns black. Take the peppers out of the oven, transfer to a freezer bag and leave for 15 minutes. Then peel off the skin with a knife and use according to the recipe.

Drain the peppers in a sieve. Peel the garlic. Coarsely chop the walnuts and toast in a dry frying pan. Finely blend all the ingredients in a blender and season with salt and pepper. It can keep in the refrigerator for about 1 week.

Serving tip: Garnish with sesame seeds and flat-leaf parsley.

LEMON AND CASHEW MOUSSE

◆

Soaked cashews are an integral part of vegan cuisine. They can be used as a substitute for cream and ricotta, and even for cheese in gratin dishes. We use them to make a fresh mousse, and we hope it convinces lacto-vegetarians of the versatility of cashew nuts. Besides having a wonderfully sweet and nutty flavour, they are an excellent source of vital minerals, such as magnesium and iron.

INGREDIENTS

Makes 300 g
Preparation time: 10 minutes plus soaking time

125 g cashew nuts
½ shallot
½ clove garlic
½ untreated lemon
¼ bunch chives
salt
white pepper

◢
Tip

The lemon and cashew mousse can keep for 2–3 days in the refrigerator.

1. Cover the cashews with water in a bowl and soak overnight. Peel the shallot and garlic. Rinse the lemon under hot water, grate a little of its zest and squeeze the juice. Wash, shake dry and finely chop the chives.

2. Combine the cashews with their soaking water, the shallot, garlic, a pinch of lemon zest and 1½ tablespoons of lemon juice in a blender and blend to a fine paste. Add water if necessary. Season with salt and pepper and incorporate the chives.

BEAN AND CAPER DIP

◆

This dip, made with two excellent sources of protein, goes
wonderfully well with a baguette loaf, as well as a glass
of red wine on the terrace...

INGREDIENTS

Makes 250 g
Preparation time: 10 minutes

1 tin haricot beans (drained weight 250 g)
½ untreated lemon
1 tsp pickled capers
3–4 sun-dried tomatoes in oil
2 tsp dried basil
3 tbsp olive oil
salt
freshly ground pepper

Drain the beans in a sieve. Squeeze the lemon.
Combine the beans, capers, tomatoes, basil and
olive oil in a blender and finely purée. Season
with salt and pepper.

Tip

If you aren't keen on capers, replace with olives. This
dip can keep for 2–3 days in the refrigerator.

BLIZZA SAUCE

◆

Our blizza sauce is made in a jiffy and is a treat not only on pizza.

INGREDIENTS

Makes 250 ml
Preparation time: 5 minutes

1 small clove garlic
½ small onion
250 g tomato passata (sieved tomatoes)
1 tsp honey or agave syrup
1 tsp Italian herbs
salt
freshly ground pepper

Peel the garlic and onion. Combine with the
passata, honey or agave syrup and Italian herbs in
a blender and finely purée. Season with salt and
pepper.

Tip

Any leftover blizza sauce can simply be heated in a
pan and enjoyed with a serving of pasta.
It can keep in the refrigerator for about 1 week.

HOT PEPPER AND CHILLI SAUCE

◆

We're big fans of Thai sriracha hot sauce.
Unfortunately, we haven't come across any to date that don't contain artificial
flavour-enhancing ingredients, so we decided to make it ourselves. Only use it
sparingly – it can hurt.

INGREDIENTS

Makes 200 ml
Preparation time: 25 minutes

200 g red chilli peppers
1 red pepper
2 cloves garlic
2 tbsp olive oil
1 tsp salt
2 tsp honey or agave syrup
2 tbsp tomato purée
50 ml white wine vinegar

◢

Tip

If you want the sauce chunkier and really fiery,
don't strain it. This hot sauce can keep for a few
weeks in the refrigerator.

1. Wash the chillies and pepper, and remove the stems, seeds and ribs. Peel the garlic and combine with the pepper and chillies in a blender and chop, or finely chop with a knife.

2. Heat the olive oil in a small saucepan and add the pepper, chilli and garlic mixture. Simmer uncovered, stirring constantly, until most of the liquid has evaporated.

3. Add the salt, honey or agave syrup, tomato purée, 30 ml of water and vinegar, and bring to the boil. Reduce for 5 minutes. Finally, strain through a fine sieve.

CHILLI AND BEAN DIP

♦

A spicy, spreadable dip that can be made quickly and easily.
We use it to make our chilli and bean rolls (see recipe on page 76).

INGREDIENTS

Makes 250 g
Preparation time: 15 minutes

400 g tin kidney beans
1 small onion
1 clove garlic
2 tbsp olive oil
2 tsp red curry paste
1 tbsp tomato purée
½ tsp curry powder
½ tsp chilli powder
salt
freshly ground pepper

◢

Tip

This dip can keep for 2–3 days in the refrigerator.

1. Drain the beans in a sieve and collect the liquid. Peel and finely chop the onion and garlic. Heat the olive oil in a small saucepan. Sweat the onion and garlic in the oil. Add the curry paste, tomato purée and spices and brown together for a few minutes. Add the beans and half of the preserving liquid and mix well.

2. Transfer to a blender and finely purée. Season with salt and pepper. You can also spice it up a little more by adding more chilli powder.

CORIANDER AND MINT CHUTNEY

◆

Lovely and cool, yet spicy. This chutney surprises with its well-complemented flavour combination.

INGREDIENTS

Makes 100 g
Preparation time: 10 minutes

2 green chilli peppers
1 handful coriander leaves
½ handful mint leaves
1 lime
1 tbsp white wine vinegar
1 tbsp olive oil
salt
freshly ground pepper

Wash the chillies and remove the seeds and ribs. Wash and shake dry the coriander and mint leaves. Squeeze the lime. Combine everything with the remaining ingredients in a blender and blend. Season with salt and pepper.

PEANUT AND GINGER DIP

◆

This dip has hints of the Far East and is a perfect match for Asian-style dishes.

INGREDIENTS

Makes 250 g
Preparation time: 15 minutes

1 clove garlic
2 cm root ginger
1 small handful coriander leaves
250 g peanut butter
3 tbsp cider vinegar
2 tbsp tamari soy sauce
2 tsp agave syrup
1 tsp cayenne pepper

Peel the garlic and ginger. Wash and shake dry the coriander leaves. Combine all the ingredients in a blender and finely purée. Gradually add 125 ml of hot water until the dip is at the desired consistency.

Tip

For a bit of crunch, you can add coarsely chopped peanuts. This dip can keep in the refrigerator for about 1 week.

Tip

If you aren't too keen on the heat of the fresh chillies, you can use mild chillies from a jar. The chutney can keep in the refrigerator for about 1 week.

AVOCADO AND GARLIC DIP

◆

*A somewhat different garlic dip. Not only does the avocado
give it a particularly creamy consistency, but it also
adds extraordinary flavour.*

INGREDIENTS
Makes 300 g
Preparation time: 15 minutes

½ bunch flat-leaf parsley
1–2 clove(s) garlic
½ avocado
250 g plain yoghurt
1 tsp white wine vinegar
salt
white pepper

Wash the parsley, shake dry and pluck the leaves. Peel and coarsely chop the garlic. Scoop out the avocado flesh. Combine the parsley, garlic and avocado with the yoghurt and vinegar in a blender and purée. Season with salt and pepper. It can keep in the refrigerator for about 2–3 days.

MUSTARD AND APRICOT DIP

◆

*This dip is really quick to make with apricot jam.
Don't be sparing with this dip, and use jam with a high fruit content.*

INGREDIENTS
Makes 100 g
Preparation time: 5 minutes

4 tbsp apricot jam
1 tsp sweet mustard
1 tsp Dijon mustard
2 tsp cider vinegar
1 tsp dried thyme

Mix all the ingredients together.

◢

Tip

This dip can keep in the refrigerator
for about 2 weeks.

For the vegan version:
Use soya yoghurt.

TOMATO AND PEPPER RELISH

◆

As a dip, sauce or spread, this relish is versatile and goes with practically everything. Best when prepared in large quantities and stored in jars.

INGREDIENTS
Makes 450 g
Preparation time: 50 minutes

400 g tomatoes
1 yellow pepper
1 onion
1 clove garlic
2 tbsp olive oil
1 tbsp tomato purée
2 tsp ground ginger
25 ml red wine
2 tsp honey or agave syrup
salt
freshly ground pepper

◢

Tip

If you want the sauce chunkier and hotter, don't strain it. This hot sauce can keep for a few weeks in the refrigerator.

1. Wash the tomatoes and the pepper. Finely dice the tomatoes. Remove the seeds from the pepper and also finely dice. Peel and finely chop the onion and garlic.

2. Heat the olive oil in a small saucepan. Sweat the onion and garlic in the oil. Incorporate the tomato purée and ground ginger, brown for a few minutes, and then deglaze with the red wine. Add the diced tomatoes and pepper together with the honey or agave syrup. Cook over a medium heat for 40 minutes, stirring often. Season with salt and pepper.

ALMOND MAYONNAISE

◆

Most vegan mayonnaise-style sauces are made using soya. Instead, we use almond butter in combination with other ingredients, leaving out the egg. It is important to use refined rapeseed oil, because it has a neutral flavour, and does not overpower the spices.

INGREDIENTS

Makes 250 g
Preparation time: 10 minutes

1 untreated lemon
2 tbsp white almond butter
1 tsp vegetable stock granules
2 tsp Dijon mustard
1 tsp turmeric
1 tsp sweet paprika
200 ml rapeseed oil
salt
freshly ground pepper

Tip

Perfect as a potato salad dressing. Simply mix with boiled and cut-up potatoes. Add chopped chives and pickled gerkhins.
Season with the gherkin pickling liquid, salt and pepper. This mayonnaise can keep in the refrigerator for about 1 week.

Halve the lemon and squeeze the juice. Combine the almond butter with 100 ml of lukewarm water, the vegetable broth granules, mustard, turmeric, paprika and lemon juice in a deep container and blend with a stick blender on the highest speed. Gradually add the oil while continuing to blend to a creamy consistency. Season with salt and pepper.

HERB AND GHERKIN REMOULADE

◆

Everybody loves remoulade. Ours offers the fresh flavours of dill, tarragon and parsley. The plain yoghurt base means it isn't as hard to digest as the conventional condiment.

INGREDIENTS
Makes 250 g
Preparation time: 10 minutes

1 small red onion
5 pickled gherkins
1 tsp fresh dill
2 tsp dried tarragon
2 tbsp flat-leaf parsley
6 tbsp mayonnaise or almond mayonnaise
  (see recipe on page 148)
125 g plain yoghurt
salt and freshly ground pepper

Peel the onion and finely chop together with the gherkins. Wash, shake dry and finely chop the herbs. Mix the mayonnaise with the yoghurt and herbs, and season with salt and pepper. It can keep in the refrigerator for about 1 week.

CURRY, MANDARIN AND RICOTTA DIP

◆

A fruity dip for lots of different occasions. Suitable for potatoes, bread and even a BBQ.

INGREDIENTS
Makes 400 g
Preparation time: 10 minutes

½ tin mandarin wedges (drained weight 315 g)
1 spring onion
125 g vegetarian ricotta cheese
125 g low-fat quark
½ tsp mild curry powder
salt and freshly ground pepper

Drain the mandarin wedges in a sieve and collect the liquid. Trim, wash and finely slice the spring onions. Mix the ricotta and quark with the curry powder and 1½ tablespoons of mandarin juice. Incorporate the spring onions and mandarin wedges, and season with salt and pepper.

For the vegan version:
Use egg-free mayonnaise
and soya yoghurt.

Tip

This dip can keep in the refrigerator for 2–3 days.
The leftover mandarin and juice can be used to
make a simple dessert for two people. Simply mix
with 150 g of vanilla pudding and 100 g of yoghurt,
and serve.

For the vegan version:
Use soya yoghurt.

Tip
Always protect pesto by covering it with oil, and keep it refrigerated. That way it will keep for several weeks.

BEETROOT AND HORSERADISH DIP

◆

These red and hot roots form a distinct combination in this refreshing dip.

INGREDIENTS
Makes 250 g
Preparation time: 10 minutes

150 g plain yoghurt
3 tsp horseradish paste
100 g (1 small) pre-cooked beetroot
salt
freshly ground pepper

Mix the yoghurt with the horseradish paste. Finely grate the beetroot and incorporate. Season with salt and pepper. It can keep in the refrigerator for about 2–3 days.

ROCKET AND PISTACHIO PESTO

◆

This pesto is made from a combination of mild rocket, spicy pistachios and refreshing lime.

INGREDIENTS
Makes 150 g
Preparation time: 15 minutes

30 g shelled pistachio nuts
30 g rocket
15 g flat-leaf parsley
1 small clove garlic
½ lime
6 tbsp olive oil
1 tsp honey or agave syrup
salt
freshly ground pepper

1. Toast the pistachios in a dry frying pan. Wash and shake dry the rocket and parsley. Peel and coarsely chop the garlic. Squeeze the lime.

2. Combine everything with the olive oil and honey or agave syrup in a blender and purée. Season with salt and pepper.

PESTO ALLA GENOVESE

◆

We don't want to modify this classic pesto. Of course, you can vary the flavour by adjusting the quantities of the ingredients, but this remains the basic Ligurian recipe.

INGREDIENTS
Makes 200 g
Preparation time: 10 minutes

30 g pine nuts
1 bunch basil
1 clove garlic
100 ml olive oil
50 g vegetarian Parmesan cheese
salt
freshly ground pepper

1. Toast the pine nuts in a dry frying pan. Remove the hard stems from the basil, and wash and shake dry. Peel the garlic. Combine everything with the olive oil in a blender and purée.

2. Finely grate the cheese and incorporate into the pesto. Season with salt and pepper.

◢

Tip

If you want to save time and effort, use frozen basil.
Toasted pine nuts have a more intense flavour, but
this step can also be left out.
Always protect pesto by covering it with oil, and
keep it refrigerated. This way it will keep for several
weeks.

MANGO AND COCONUT SAUCE

◆

Sunshine, turquoise water and endless beaches... unfortunately, these we can't offer. But we can offer a recipe that is perfect for this setting and quick and easy to prepare.

INGREDIENTS

Makes 250 ml
Preparation time: 10 minutes

1 mango
1 red chilli pepper
1 clove garlic
1 cm root ginger
1 tsp tamari soy sauce
2 tbsp coconut milk
salt

Peel the mango. Remove the flesh from around the stone and cut into coarse chunks. Wash the chilli pepper, then halve and remove the stem and seeds. Peel the garlic. Peel and finely grate the ginger. Finely purée all the ingredients in a blender and season with salt.

Tip

You can use the leftover coconut milk the next day to make the lentil dahl burrito (see recipe on page 34). This sauce can keep in the refrigerator for 2–3 days.

BREAD ROLLS ETC.

Although it's faster and easier to use bread bought directly from a bakery, we'd also like to offer you the opportunity to make basic things yourself.

We have attempted to keep time-consuming steps to a minimum. It's advisable to use the breads made this way straight out of the oven as they dry out quickly. If you have time, you should normally rest dough for 1 hour after kneading, before working it again.

Our bread recipes all use wheat flour, but we leave the choice of type of flour and flavour to your taste. The amount of water required will vary depending on this. If the dough is too wet, simply add flour, and if it's too dry, add water.

ALL-PURPOSE DOUGH

◆

One dough for practically everything? Of course! We make it simple and avoid having to make small changes. Whether it's for tarte flambée, pizza or pitas, this recipe can be used for all of them. And the dough is proved in the oven, so you save valuable time.

INGREDIENTS
Makes 1 serving
Preparation time: 10 minutes

½ cube fresh yeast
250 g wheat flour
½ tsp raw cane sugar
1 tsp salt
2 tbsp olive oil

1. Crumble the yeast into a measuring cup with 125 ml of lukewarm water and stir well. Combine the flour, sugar, salt, olive oil and dissolved yeast in the bowl of a stand mixer fitted with a dough hook. Start mixing on low speed, and then gradually increase the speed to the highest setting until a smooth and even dough forms. The best way to knead dough is by hand. It takes a little practice, although not too much, but this part is the most fun.

2. Then continue with the specific recipe.

Tip

The dough can be made in large quantities and frozen. This saves on time and hassle. Simply put the proved dough into a freezer bag and into the freezer. It should keep for up to 6 months. When needed, leave it to thaw and rise overnight in the refrigerator or a covered bowl.

WHEAT TORTILLAS

◆

Once you try homemade tortillas, you won't ever want to do without them.

INGREDIENTS
Makes 6
Preparation time: 50 minutes

350 g wheat flour
180 ml water
1 tsp salt
6 tbsp olive oil

1. Combine the flour, water and salt in a large bowl and work into a smooth dough. Leave to rest for 30 minutes.

2. Divide the dough ball into six uniform pieces and roll out over a floured work surface into thin discs.

3. Heat 1 tablespoon of olive oil in a non-stick frying pan. Fry a disc over a high heat for about 1 minute on both sides until bubbles start to form in the dough. Be careful not to let the tortilla become crispy. Do the same for the other tortillas.

HERB PITAS

◆

There are countless creative possibilities for using this convenient type of flatbread. The herbs give the bread a wonderful and inviting Mediterranean flavour, even if they're only going to be enjoyed with a dip.

INGREDIENTS
Makes 4
Preparation time: 45 minutes

1 serving all-purpose dough (see recipe on page 161)
2 tbsp olive oil
2 tsp dried Italian herbs

1. Preheat the oven to 90°C (fan)/gas ¼. Divide the dough ball into four pieces and roll out over a floured work surface into palm-sized discs about 1 cm thick. Brush with olive oil and sprinkle with Italian herbs.

2. Turn off the oven. Lay the discs on a baking tray lined with parchment paper and put into the oven together with an ovenproof bowl filled with water. Leave to prove for 20 minutes. Raise the oven temperature to 220°C (fan)/gas 9 and bake for 15 minutes.

◢

Tip
You can also use fresh herbs.
In this case, brush the baked pitas with olive oil and
sprinkle with finely chopped herbs.

FLATBREAD

◆

Flatbread is the world's most commonly eaten form of bread. We make it in the same style as that used in Turkish kebab shops using a leavened dough with sesame and nigella seeds. The topping can naturally be varied to your taste.

INGREDIENTS
Makes 2 (diameter 20 cm)
Preparation time: 50 minutes

1 serving all-purpose dough (see recipe on page 161)
1 tbsp olive oil
1 tsp nigella seeds
1 tsp sesame seeds

1. Preheat the oven to 90°C (fan)/gas ¼. Halve the dough ball and use your hands to form flatbreads about 2 cm thick. The best way is to turn the dough in your hands like a steering wheel and carefully stretch. Brush with olive oil and sprinkle with sesame and nigella seeds.

2. Turn off the oven. Lay the discs on a baking tray lined with parchment paper and put into the oven together with an ovenproof bowl filled with water. Leave to prove for 20 minutes. Raise the oven temperature to 220°C (fan)/gas 9 and bake for 20 minutes.

◢

Tip

If you like a soft crust, cover the flatbread with a
damp cloth for a short time after baking.

BURGER BUNS

◆

Opinions vary on the subject of burger buns. Some like them soft and airy, while others prefer them wholegrain and firm. We try to make it right for everybody, so we've decided on a happy medium.

INGREDIENTS

Makes 4
Preparation time: 50 minutes

1 serving all-purpose dough (see recipe on page 161)
2 tbsp olive oil
2 tsp sesame seeds

1. Preheat the oven to 90°C (fan)/gas ¼. Divide the dough into four uniform pieces. Roll each piece into a ball and flatten to a thickness of about 2½ cm. Brush with olive oil and sprinkle with sesame seeds.

2. Turn off the oven. Lay the discs on a baking tray lined with parchment paper and put into the oven together with an ovenproof bowl filled with water. Leave to prove for 20 minutes. Raise the oven temperature to 220°C(fan)/gas 9 and bake for 20 minutes.

◢
Tip

If you like a soft crust, cover the burger buns with a
damp cloth for a short time after baking.

LYE ROLLS

◆

You need a little more patience for lye rolls. Here you have to prove the dough as usual so that the rolls won't collapse in the lye bath. The result: light and airy on the inside and crispy on the outside.

INGREDIENTS

Makes 4
Preparation time: 70 minutes

1 serving all-purpose dough (see recipe on page 161)
2 tbsp salt
30 g baking soda

1. Preheat the oven to 90°C (fan)/gas ¼. Put the dough ball into a bowl and cover with a cloth.

2. Turn off the oven but leave the oven light on. Prove the dough in the oven for 20 minutes. Take the dough out, knead for a few minutes and cut into four uniform pieces. Roll into balls and flatten into ovals with a thickness of 2–3 cm. Lay the rolls over a baking tray lined with parchment paper and return to the oven to prove for 15 minutes with the oven light still on.

3. In the meantime, bring 1 litre of water to the boil in a large pot. Add the salt and baking soda. Do this carefully because the water will froth up vigorously. Take the tray out of the oven. Preheat the oven to 220°C (fan)/gas 9.

4. Carefully place the rolls in the boiling water and leave for 30 seconds on each side. Use a slotted spoon to take the rolls out of the bath. Drain and return to the baking tray. Bake in the oven for 15 minutes until done.

◢

Tip

NB: shop-bought lye breads are often made with lard. Ask about this when buying them.

BAGELS

◆

These round bread rings look firm on the outside but are soft on the inside. They need to be soaked in a water bath for a short time, and like the lye rolls, need longer proving.

INGREDIENTS
Makes 4 bagels
Preparation time: 50 minutes

1 serving all-purpose dough (see recipe on page 161)
bagel toppings (e.g. sesame, poppy or pumpkin seeds)

1. Preheat the oven to 90°C (fan)/gas ¼. Put the dough ball into a bowl and cover with a cloth.

2. Turn off the oven but leave the oven light on. Prove the dough in the oven for 20 minutes. Take the dough out, knead for a few minutes and cut into four uniform pieces. Roll into balls. Pierce the middle with your forefinger, and turn the dough around your finger to make the hole bigger. The holes should have a 5–6-cm diameter, as the dough is still to rise more vigorously.

3. Lay the bagels on a baking tray lined with parchment paper and put into the oven. Return to the oven to prove for 15 minutes with the oven light still on. In the meantime, bring 1 litre of water to the boil in a large pot.

4. Take the trays out of the oven. Preheat the oven to 220°C (fan)/gas 9. Carefully place the bagels in the boiling water and leave for about 1 minute on each side. Use a slotted spoon to take the bagels out of the bath. Drain and return to the baking tray. Depending on your preference, sprinkle with sesame, poppy or pumpkin seeds, or with cheese. Bake in the oven for 17 minutes until done.

TOASTING BREAD

Why buy bread to toast when you can easily make it yourself?
With our all-purpose dough and a little patience, you can have the smell of
freshly baked bread in no time. And with a flavour that is in no way inferior to
that of shop-brought bread.

INGREDIENTS

For a 24-cm baking tin
Preparation time: 1 hour 15 minutes

2 servings all-purpose dough (see recipe on page 161)
50 g margarine

1. Preheat the oven to 90°C (fan)/gas ¼. Prepare the all-purpose dough ball, but instead of kneading olive oil into the dough, use 50 g of soft margarine.

2. Turn off the oven. Grease the baking tin with margarine and fill with the dough. Put into the oven together with an ovenproof bowl filled with water.
Leave to prove for 20 minutes. Then heat the oven to 200°C (fan)/gas 7. Bake for 45 minutes, then take out of the oven. Knock on the loaf with your fist: if it sounds hollow, the bread is ready.

Tip

If you like a soft crust, cover the loaf with a damp cloth for a short time after baking.

DRINKS ETC.

Decent fast food also needs the right drink.

Lemonade and cola are naturally the first things to
come to mind. So we offer two exceptionally refreshing
recipes.

LEMON GINGERADE

There's no reason why lemonade should be unhealthy. This version contains a lot of sugar, but also a lot of vitamin C, working together with the goodness of ginger to strengthen the immune system.

INGREDIENTS
Makes about 500 ml
Preparation time: 15 minutes

100 g root ginger
2 untreated lemons
100 g raw cane sugar

1. Peel the ginger. Rinse the lemons under hot water. Cut the ginger and lemons into coarse chunks and blend with 250 ml of water in a blender.

2. Combine the sugar with 100 ml of water in a small saucepan and cook to a syrup over a low heat while stirring constantly. Once the sugar has dissolved, wrap the lemon and ginger mixture in a clean cloth and squeeze the liquid into the syrup. Leave to cool.

3. Dilute with soda water and serve.

Serving tip: Serve with finely chopped mint.

SPICE COLA

Now you don't have to look too hard to find what was for a very long time the top secret recipe for the black soda drink with red and white lettering on the Internet. But with so many ingredients, it's too complicated for us. By simplifying, it tastes just as good, if not better.

INGREDIENTS
Makes about 500 ml
Preparation time: 45 minutes

2 untreated oranges
2 untreated limes
3 cm root ginger
4 cm vanilla pod
1 point star anise
2 cloves
½ tsp ground cardamom
1 pinch ground cinnamon
200 g raw cane sugar

1. For the spice liquid, wash the oranges and limes under hot water. Remove the zest with a vegetable peeler, finely chop and put into a small saucepan. Squeeze the juice and top up with 500 ml of water. Peel and finely slice the ginger. Split the vanilla pod and crush the star anise point. Combine everything with the cloves, cardamom, cinnamon and orange and lime juice, bring to the boil and simmer for 15 minutes.

2. In the meantime, put the sugar in another saucepan over a medium heat and slowly caramelise, stirring constantly until it is liquid and slightly brownish. Remove from the heat. Strain the spice liquid through a sieve into the caramelised sugar. Do this carefully because it will splash and foam up. Continue to stir until the sugar is completely dissolved.

3. Fill a clean, swing-top glass bottle and leave to cool. Dilute with soda water and serve.

Recipe index

Keyword index

Acknowledgements

Many thanks!

As with all books, there are a large number of people besides the author who are involved in production. We would like to use this page to mention and thank the people who worked on this book.

We would first like to thank Katharina and Uschi, the recipe tasters who bravely tried out the different dishes and who were able to identify any errors. We would also like to thank everybody who had offered to help with the testing and whom we were unable to consider. ☺
Special thanks to our parents, who went to so much trouble to take care of so many essential things, and who made so much room for us so that we could work on the book.

We thank our young daughter Carla, who made the effort of going to bed early so that we could have time to cook. And we especially thank her for each of the many wonderful moments she gives us and for encouraging us to enjoy our lives every day.

We would like to thank Marion for her incredible help and support with the reports and for helping us through our inexperience with paperwork.

Our well-deserved thanks go to Franzi for the beautiful design and the efforts that went into it.

We would like to thank Christian Verlag, especially Annemarie Heinel, for giving us the exciting opportunity to be able to publish this book.

And, last but not least, many thanks to you for buying our book and for your interest. We hope you haven't been disappointed, and that you have the chance to enjoy the recipes in it on many occasions.

Published in 2016 by
Grub Street
4 Rainham Close
London
SW11 6SS

Email: food@grubstreet.co.uk
Web: www.grubstreet.co.uk
Twitter: @grub_street
Facebook: Grub Street Publishing

Layout and type: Franziska Detlof
Illustration: Franziska Detlof
Text and recipes: Clarissa and Florian Sehn
Food styling: Fotobrinkops Team
Photography: Maria Brinkop
All photographs were taken by Maria Brinkop, except on page 6 taken by Patrick Pees

A CIP catalogue record for this book is available from the British Library.

ISBN 978-1-910690-18-5

Printed and bound by Finidr, Czech Republic.

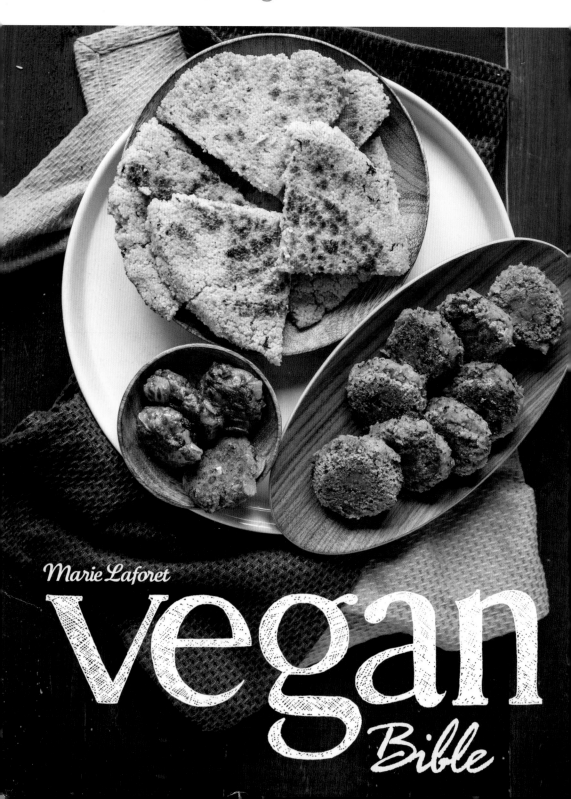

Marie Laforet

vegan
Bible

VEGETARIAN
COOKING
Step *by* Step

Lena Tritto